"Daybreak Devotions"

A devotion for life's emotions

By

Dawn Glaser

Daybreak Devotions, a devotion for life's emotions
by Dawn Glaser
Edited by Liz Mabie
Published by: Yawn's Publishing
210 East Main Street
Canton, GA 30114
www.yawnspublishing.com

Library of Congress Control Number: 2012953762

ISBN: 978-1-936815-74-6

Printed in the United States of America.

Foreword

"I truly believe God has shown us a living, breathing miracle – the miracle of a life redeemed by Christ. Like many of us, Dawn has experienced the fate of trying to control her own destiny only to return to the God who loves her and wants only the best for her. Our Lord perfectly places her right in the midst of hospital patients, abortion recovery ministries and with women who have experienced sexual abuse. He does this because Dawn knows something that many do not – that God is faithful and that Jesus saves. She understands He came and died for all and that no sin is beyond redemption. Dawn boldly shares this message with all who will hear it."

Jamie K. Williams, CFP®, CLTC
Five Talents Wealth Management, Inc.

Acknowledgements

I want to thank God first and foremost for giving me the inspirations and vision to write a ninety day devotional book. I pray that it will help others get through their day and reflect on the one true God who is Holy, Worthy, and can bless their life abundantly as he has mine through his son, Jesus!

With special thanks, I want to thank my husband, Chris, for your love and support. When I couldn't think of a topic to write about, you always helped me think of one and then the words would just flow from there. When I wanted to give up, you encouraged me. I love you so much! I want to thank my two boys, Preston and Adam. Thank you for lending your ears while I read to you so many of these devotions! I am so grateful for the journey that God laid out before me when he gave me the gift of each of you. I pray that you will take some nuggets of wisdom that I learned from others along the way and as you grow older will apply them to your life, marriage, and family. I love all of you more than you realize. You are my light that keeps me going! I want to thank my publisher, Nadine Yawn with Yawn's Publishing for publishing this book and giving me a chance so that others can be blessed! I want to thank Liz Mabie for your gift and talent in editing this book. I am forever grateful to you my sister in Christ for your wisdom! God sent you and you showed up! Thank you for my friends and family for your encouragement, love, and support! Without you, this book would only be just a vision. I owe everything I have to God, my family, and the people he placed in my pathway who made this book possible! I pray that it will touch the hearts of many.

Psalm 5:3 *In the morning Lord, you hear my voice; In the morning, I lay my request before you and wait expectantly.*

The Way to Jesus Christ Our Lord is Simple:

1) Admit that you are a Sinner and need a Savior. Romans 3:23 For all have sinned and come short of the glory of God.

2) Believe that Jesus Christ is God the Son who paid your sin debt in full at the Cross was dead and buried and resurrected on the third day and ascended into Heaven to prepare a place for you. Romans 6:23 For the wages of sin is death but the gift of God is eternal life through Jesus Christ our Lord.

3) Cry out to God and ask Him to take control of your life and come into your heart and change your mind in order to live for Him. Romans 10:9 If thou shalt confess with thy mouth the Lord Jesus, and shalt believe in thine heart that God hath raised him from the dead, thou shalt be saved.

After you realize you need Jesus in your life and ask him to come into your heart and change you then He will. (1 Corinthians 3:16) He will slowly transform you into His likeness and for His purpose, which is to glorify Him and Him alone. You will need to put Him first in your life above all else. Read His word daily, pray, and turn from your old ways. This life is temporary, and we are only passing through. Whatever you do in life, make sure it has an "eternal impact" for God's Glory and you will never go wrong!

Blessings!

Contents

Patience

Learning to Listen

Lately I have been struggling with Patience and Self Control. I have always just gone full speed ahead with anything I have ever been passionate about. I am learning that in that process I have not chosen to fully wait upon the Lord for His answer and clarity. What I think is a confirmation from Him may be the "devil in disguise" waiting in the wings to pounce on my parade! Galatians 5:22 -23 says,"But the fruit of the Spirit is love, joy, peace, forbearance, kindness, goodness, faithfulness, gentleness and self-control. Against such things there is no law." Colossians 3:12 states: Therefore, as God's chosen people, holy and dearly loved, clothe yourselves with compassion, kindness, humility, gentleness, and patience. Ouch! I truly need help in this department Lord! I can't wait for the water in the pot to boil, much less wait on something HUGE in my life! I am praying about this and if you are having a hard time with it, I hope you are to. For me it will take a lot of prayer. Charles Spurgeon once wrote, "Patience is the companion of wisdom." Today I purposely told my children I had lost my voice. I instantly began to think of Zechariah in the bible that God made him lose his voice to teach him obedience and patience for lack of his faith. I have the faith but lack in the patience. Anyway, I was able to spend time with my children and hear them talk and say things that I needed to hear. Usually I sing very loud in the car but today in the car, I didn't sing at all. Instead, I got to listen to my son enjoy the music and tap to the beat. Are you speaking too much and missing what others are trying to tell you? Are you like me and your just so excited that you talk out of turn, speak before thinking, and miss what God is trying to tell you? Forgive me Father. Slow me down so that I can hear your still small voice and encounter the emotions of your heart.

Prayer for today: *Father in Heaven, teach me to be so in tune with you that I can always hear the whisper of your voice in my ear. In Jesus' name, Amen.*

Being Still

I have never been one to sit still. I get that I think from my mom. She is a busybody and so I am I. She recently retired last week and this week she has opened up her own business. I knew she wouldn't stay retired for long. My husband tells me often that I should relax and rest more. That's easy for someone if they have the makeup of a person who doesn't have a care in the world. I get up early each day and try to see how much I can cram into my day and be productive. I honestly think I would have enjoyed living in the 1800's on a farm. I can imagine getting up early and milking the cow, gathering the eggs, and finding time to can jellies and jams. If you've never canned before the process

Patience

takes a while. While doing so you have to boil the jars, lids, seals and it requires a lot of stirring and a lot of waiting. When making jelly preserves you have to skim off the impurities off the top so that when it's in the jar it will look pretty. To me that's how God is processing our lives. If we would just sit still long enough to hear him speaking to us he would skim off the impurities found within us. I love the verse in Psalms 46:10. It says the following: Be still and know that I am God. How many times have we been so busy that we don't sit still and wait on the Lord for an answer? I am learning to do that now. I am over 40 years old and if I had only known to do that in my earlier years I would have saved myself a lot of heartache. Often times I have been too busy to wait upon the Lord. It involves a lot of patience and self control. Being still requires being quiet long enough to be able to listen. In Isaiah 30:15, it says the following: In quietness and confidence shall be your strength. Are you taking time out each day to be still long enough to hear God speaking to you? If you're like me sometimes and have to pencil him in your schedule then you are too busy. Satan wants you to be so busy that you don't have time for God. It's time to make time for God and be still.

Prayer for today: *Heavenly Father, Please help me with patience and learning to wait upon you and your timing. In Jesus' name, Amen.*

Memory Overload

When your computer doesn't have any space for memory then it's time to reboot it and start over. The same thing happens with our mind. Sometimes it gets so filled up with junk, that there is not any room left for God. When you start your day, clutter enters your mind with your surroundings, and we often allow it to happen. On the news, you can hear about a car fire, a robbery, and an injury of some kind every single day of the week. If you're a mom when you hear the kids asking a hundred questions, the dog barking, keeping up with schedules, the phone ringing, your spouse wanting to know what's for dinner, then it's easy for you to scream! It sometimes can put your brain much like the computer into memory space overload! If you're a dad, and your worried because the blackberry is filled up with deadlines, your emails are full, the bills need to be paid, you're stuck in rush hour and don't have enough time in the day to spend with your family, then your brain needs rebooting! I have been known for counting to ten backwards often in order to regroup my thoughts. How can we hear God speak to us, when there is so much noise? He wants us to come to the quiet. In the book of Acts Chapter 16 in the Bible, it talks about Paul preaching to women in Philippi at the river. A woman named, Lydia was listening. God spoke to her heart and she invited Paul and his followers into to her home. She was a true worshiper of God and was so in tune with him that when he spoke to her she was obedient, listened, and followed through with what God wanted her to do. If her mind had been focused on selling her purple cloth for the day and making money, she would have missed out on an opportunity God had planned for her. In Jeremiah 17:10 it says the following: "I the Lord search the heart and examine the mind, to reward each person according to their conduct, according to what their deeds deserve." in Ezekiel 11:5 it says the following: Then the Spirit of the Lord came on me, and he told me to say: "This is what the Lord says: That is what you are saying, you leaders in Israel, but I know what is going through your mind. If we choose to fill our minds with clutter then He knows it. Are you meditating on his word? Are you praying to him with everything that concerns you? Or are you almost out of memory and need to be rebooted? One verse in the morning will not sustain me through my entire day. I need to hear from God through his spirit, his music, his word all day long in order to function. My memory has plenty of files that need cleaning up daily to make room for our Lord. Doesn't yours?

Prayer for today: *Heavenly Father, I pray that you will always fill my mind with your word through scripture, song, and others. In Jesus' name, Amen.*

Slow Me Down Lord

Today is the day the Lord is slowing me down. I am scheduled to have surgery in just a few hours. The things women go through! They have told me

no bending, no lifting, no driving, and certainly not to tear the stitches. So what is one suppose to do for six to eight weeks?

I think God knows I am the perfect carbon copy of my mother. I am always busy. I feel like if I am not "doing", then I am not productive. I enjoy staying busy with keeping up with my family, errands, and volunteering. Sometimes though I over do it and that is probably why, God is making me rest. I will have no choice but to slow down and pray, study his word, and listen to Him. I confess, I am a Martha! Martha was a busybody too. She couldn't see Jesus for worrying and cleaning! Can you relate? In Luke 10:32-48 the Bible says the following: As Jesus and his disciples were on their way, he came to a village where a woman named Martha opened her home to him. She had a sister called Mary, who sat at the Lord's feet listening to what he said. But Martha was distracted by all the preparations that had to be made. She came to him and asked, "Lord, don't you care that my sister has left me to do the work by myself? Tell her to help me!"

"Martha, Martha," the Lord answered, "you are worried and upset about many things, but few things are needed—or indeed only one. Mary has chosen what is better, and it will not be taken away from her." Ouch! It sounds like Martha was so worried about her house, she missed out on Jesus being in her own living room! Wow! Did you know He is in every room of your house every day? Haven't you seen that saying that says: I the Lord your God am the silent listener and present at every conversation. Well, if you haven't it's hanging in my kitchen as a reminder. I am guilty. I have put the computer, friends, television, and being busy first above God. He's saying "Dawn, Dawn", you are worried about many things, but I am what matters most. Now rest in me and learn to slow down.

Prayer for today: *Father God, forgive me for not putting you first above everything. I pray that my surgery is in your hands today and will go exactly as you have planned. I thank you for teaching me how to be more like Mary and not so much like Martha so I can benefit from listening to you. In Jesus' name, Amen.*

Let's Go Fishing

I can think back to when I was around ten years old and remember going fishing with my Nanny and

Paw Paw. Nanny would pack the best ham and cheese biscuits to take along. I loved fishing with a cane pole. Paw Paw had a worm bed as he called it and would scoop up a good handful to take along. We would walk down the windy dirt road behind their house to the pond and then once we arrived, I was instructed to keep my mouth shut and sit and wait. I think Nanny would let me have the biscuits early so I would do just that. That was the hardest part of the trip for me. Sitting and waiting. Over this past summer I had a friend challenge me to pick one chapter out of the Bible and read it, study it, and breathe it. God laid it on my heart, to read about Job. If there is anyone who had to sit and wait and be patient in the Bible, it was Job. God allowed Satan to test Job in order to try his patience and see how obedient and faithful he would remain to God. In Job 42:12 it says: The Lord blessed the latter part of Job's life more than the first. He had fourteen thousand sheep, six thousand camels, a thousand yoke of oxen and a thousand donkeys. God blessed him for waiting and sticking it out. There was a lot of God waiters now that I think about it. Take a look at Noah. Noah waited on the Lord 120 years as it took him that long to build the ark! Can you imagine? Noah lived 350 years "after" the flood! Puts a whole new meaning to Isaiah 40:31 that says: "But they that wait upon the LORD shall renew their strength; they shall mount up with wings as eagles; they shall run, and not be weary; and they shall walk, and not faint". God made Moses wait for the appointed time to bring his people out of Egypt. Any sooner and God would not

Patience

have been glorified. God made Hannah wait for a son. 1 Samuel 2:19-21 it says: May The Lord give you children by this woman to take the place of the one she prayed for and gave to The Lord." Then they would go home. And The Lord was gracious to Hannah; she conceived and gave birth to three sons and two daughters. Meanwhile, the boy Samuel grew up in the presence of The Lord. God showed favor on Hannah for waiting. God made Joseph wait for his brothers at just the right time and then God was glorified. In Psalm 37:34,9 it says the following: Wait on the LORD, and keep His way, and He shall exalt thee to inherit the land: when the wicked are cut off, thou shalt see it. For evildoers shall be cut off: but those that wait upon the LORD, they shall inherit the earth. All of these God Waiters trusted in the Lord and waited for His perfect timing. God is teaching me patience and trust in learning to wait. Just as when I was little with my grandparents and had wait on that bobbin to go under the water without saying a word, sitting still, and keeping my mouth shut I am learning to do the same with God.

Prayer for today: *Heavenly Father, thank you for slowing me down long enough to pray, wait, and listen for your word. May you continue to slow me down so that I can be so in tune with you that I hear your voice. In Jesus' name, Amen.*

Early Riser

It is 4:58 a.m. and I am wide awake. This morning the first thing on my mind was a song called, "Courageous" by Casting Crowns. Usually nine times out of ten some kind of song comes to mind or I hear God speak something to me. Then I think about what or who I need to be in prayer for and go pray. I then start my morning routine before the rest of my family wakes up. I take our dog out, start my coffee, and grab my Bible and devotional books. Now there are times on occasion when I am thrown off schedule and have to spend my time with God at a different time. If that happens, it seems my whole day is thrown off. Do you take out time for God? What does the bible say about spending time with him? In Micah 6:8 it says the following: He has shown you, O mortal, what is good. In addition, what does the Lord require of you? To act justly and to love mercy and to walk humbly with your God. If we walk with God daily, then He will carry us through the day a whole lot easier than without him. We will be prepared to handle a crisis when one comes up unexpectedly. In Isaiah 43:2, it says the following: When you pass through the waters, I will be with you; and when you pass through the rivers, they will not sweep over you. When you walk through the fire, you will not be burned; the flames will not set you ablaze.

I know when I miss my time with him; somehow my day goes by out of order. I lose patience, love, and good character qualities that he may have reminded me of that I may have needed

Patience

that day had I spent time with him. If we start our day with noise, television, and the phone, our day immediately turns into so many things that fill your mind that there is no room for God. If you have a hard time waking up early, pray about it. Ask God to wake you up so that you can hear what he wants to tell you. You know Jesus did a lot of praying. He made it a point to spend time alone with God. In Luke 5:16 it says the following: But Jesus often withdrew to lonely places and prayed. God is waiting to hear from you. Won't you start off your day pleasing him, so that he can delight in you?

Prayer for today: *Heavenly Father, I pray that you will always wake me up to spend time with you in the mornings Lord. I cherish that time with you and you alone and am grateful for the relationship with you that starts my day right! In Jesus' name, Amen.*

Obedient

Kept Alive

While watering my flowers yesterday I looked over to water my plant that my grandmother gave me before she died. I was amazed at the thought of how the plant has lived so long! You see when my grandmother got married to my grandfather her mother gave her this plant as a wedding gift in 1932. For 52 years that she was married to my grandfather, she kept the plant alive. She watered it, she gave it the tender, loving, care that it needed, and plant food weekly in order to survive. After my grandfather passed away, she continued to nourish that plant for another twenty-two years before she went home to Heaven. Two weeks prior to her passing, I went to visit her and she wanted to give me the plant. I said, " Nanny I don't have a green thumb is you sure you want me to have it?" She said to water it twice a week and it would be fine. Well, guess what, so far so good. I am amazed that I haven't let her down.

When thinking of the plant I also was thinking about our mind and body and how we stay alive in relation to the plant. You see it made me think that once you've accepted Christ as your savior you have to take care of your body with the proper nourishment that it needs because your body is the temple where Jesus resides. You also have to water your mind daily with His living water and saturate it with His word. In doing so you will keep the enemy at bay and stamp Gods word on your heart and in your mind, so that you can retain it. When you go into battle with a crisis just like the plant in the boiling sun and heat of the day the water protects it just as Gods living water does for you. The word of God speaks of water 722 times throughout the bible. It speaks of purification of the Christian. It speaks of water as spiritual life to the Christian. In the book of Genesis 1:2, the scripture first mentions the word water, and how God hovered over it. In Ephesians 5:6, it talks about how we might be cleansed, by the washing of the water of the word. In John 4:14 it talks about how you will never thirst if you stay in His word. In addition, in Revelation it says how if you come to Him take the water of life freely. Do you want to be kept alive? Do you want to live forever? Do you want to never have to go thirsty in the noonday sun? Then simply get in God's word daily and saturate your very soul.

Prayer for today: *Heavenly Father, May I continue to draw near to you as you do to me. May I always thirst for your living water yet never go thirsty. In Jesus' name, Amen.*

Play by the Rules

Have you ever felt like something was not worth the trouble? Having a child with a life threatening illness always throws up a red flag. Sometimes I really get tired of our public school

13

system. Every year I have to have forms completed by my son's doctors for a homebound teacher in case we need one. I also have to meet with all of his teachers and counselor to complete more forms pertaining to his health background and limitations. If sports are involved then that separate amount of forms has to be completed. I also have to type up a letter stating my son's health restrictions and get a letter from his doctor stating the same thing. Are these forms the same as last years? Yes, they are and he has had the same diagnosis since he was four years old. He is now going to be a junior in high school and we have to still go through the same routine year after year. The reason we are told we have to go through the same agenda every year boils down to rules. The word obey was first mentioned to Abraham in the bible by God in Genesis 22:17, 18. Because Abraham obeyed Gods voice, God blessed him. In Deuteronomy, the word command is mentioned seventy-seven times and the word commandment is mentioned forty-three times. God demanded obedience. I know when God passed down the Ten Commandments through Moses the Israelites didn't want to abide by those rules. I don't like the rules either. I want to change things up and make up my own rules sometimes. If I did that, though I would not be obeying those in authority. In Hebrews 13:17 it says: Have confidence in your leaders and submit to their authority, because they keep watch over you as those who must give an account. Do this so that their work will be a joy, not a burden, for that would be of no benefit to you. When we are driving

Obedient

under the speed limit, we are obeying those in authority. When we are following the rules of our employer, we are obeying authority. When we follow, Gods will; we are obeying God. In the book of Matthew 22:37-39 Jesus replied: "Love the Lord your God with all your heart and with all your soul and with your entire mind. This is the first and greatest commandment. In addition, the second is like it: 'Love your neighbor as yourself. Our neighbor to me would include everyone you meet, red, yellow, black or white as well as our peers, teachers, parents, and our employer. Jesus didn't say you get to pick and choose. He said love with everything you've got, with all that you have, and without excuse. If we are to follow the rules then we must play the game correctly or we will lose every time.

Prayer for today: *Heavenly Father, Please help me obey authority and know that I must set a good example in doing so. Forgive me of my shortcomings and help me be a stronger person for your will. In Jesus' name, Amen.*

Success in a System

I rarely watch television anymore, but yesterday while doing laundry I chose to. As I was watching, a commercial came on for a diet plan. The celebrity talked of how you could have a body like hers in no time with their "system". She made it sound fun, easy and affordable. Catchy, I thought, however that's not for me. Their idea is sending you

Obedient

meals in a box that are of little proportion, and the pounds just happen to fall off. Then wham! Just like that, you will be a success! I think not. What happens when they stop sending the meals? You really would have to discipline yourself right? What does it take to make YOU a success? If you chose Hollywood actors and actresses, would you think they were successful? Most end in divorce, marry several times, have a drug or drinking problem, end up in rehab, and the only thing that defines them of their success is their money. I have a different view on that topic. It's one that is spiritual. In Genesis 27:20 Isaac asked his son, "How did you find it so quickly, my son?" "The LORD your God gave me success," he replied. Joshua 1:7 "Be strong and very courageous. Be careful to obey all the law my servant Moses gave you; do not turn from it to the right or to the left, that you may be successful wherever you go." Joshua 1:8 says " Keep this Book of the Law always on your lips; meditate on it day and night, so that you may be careful to do everything written in it. Then you will be prosperous and successful." 1 Samuel 18:14 says "In everything he did he had great success, because the LORD was with him." Proverbs 2:7 says "He holds success in store for the upright, he is a shield to those whose walk is blameless," Daniel 11:36 says "The king will do as he pleases. He will exalt and magnify himself above every god and will say unheard-of things against the God of gods. He will be successful until the time of wrath is completed, for what has been determined must take place." 1 Chronicles 22:13 says "Then you will have success if you are careful to observe the decrees and laws that the LORD gave Moses for Israel. Be strong and courageous. Do not be afraid or discouraged."

To me, all of these verses say that if we meditate on God's word, be strong and courageous, walk with him daily and stay in His will for our life, then we will be successful. In order to do those things, however, you must have the Holy Spirit inside of you to lead you and be your guide. Adrian Rogers once wrote "It's not necessarily being famous, not necessarily being wealthy or healthy, but success is the progressive realization of the goal of God for your life." That reminds me of an old church hymn that I still hear from time to time. "Trust and Obey." some of the lyrics are as follows:

When we walk with the Lord in the light of His Word, What a glory He sheds on our way! While we do His good will, He abides with us still, And with all who will trust and obey.

If we just trust and obey, we will be successful! That's the system that works! It's His way!

Prayer for today: *Heavenly Father, may You continue to use me and direct my paths. Take away any fear from the enemy and help me to be strong and courageous. Help me to retain Your word within me so I can take it wherever I go and be successful in Your eyes. In Jesus' name, Amen.*

Wake up Call

Take a look around you. No, take a good long look. Our society is in a hurry, wants everything easy and it's as if no one realizes what their purpose in life is or why they are here. Is it to have friends and party? Is it to find the man or woman of your dreams? Is it to one day get that huge dream house, car or boat? What about climbing the ladder to the top of the company or taking that cruise or flight to a getaway island? In Hollywood, it's common that if a relationship does not work out, it's ok to find someone else. This is not God's plan or prescription for marriage at all. Our society without God has no direction. We look to others for answers rather than the one book that has them all, which is God's Holy Word. When things are going well without God (so it may seem) eventually you are going to go through some rough waters. When the waters get rough, then fear sets in. The enemy surrounds you, and unless you have God as your anchor, you will sink. Sometimes God allows bad things to happen to get our attention. Sometimes He sends a wakeup call to get your attention before it's too late.

In Genesis 6:13 it says "So God said to Noah, 'I am going to put an end to all people, for the earth is filled with violence because of them. I am surely going to destroy both them and the earth.'" Noah built an ark and was saved from the great flood because he lived an upright, blameless life and God granted him favor. God not only used people as an example, He also often used to warn the people to change their ways or they would feel his wrath. He

Obedient

told Jonah to warn the town of Nineveh. In Jonah 3:4 it says "Jonah began by going a day's journey into the city, proclaiming, 'Forty more days and Nineveh will be overthrown.'" Jeremiah 1:7-8 says "But the Lord said to me, 'Do not say, 'I am too young.' You must go to everyone I send you to and say whatever I command you. Do not be afraid of them, for I am with you and will rescue you,'" declares the Lord.

What would it take for God to get your attention so that you would put Him first in your life above all else? Would He have to flood the earth? Would He have to send a messenger? Would He have to take whatever or whomever away from you as a wakeup call? Charles Spurgeon once wrote "It is high time that you should awake out of sleep, for now is your damnation nearer than when you first heard the Gospel and rejected it." Take heed, take heed! God grant you Grace to take heed and to believe in Christ. Amen and Amen!

Prayer for today: *Heavenly Father, I pray today that those that are dear to me and even those whom I do not know will wake up to Your calling before it's too late. I pray for those whose lives are attacked by the enemy, that they would seek refuge in You and You alone. In Jesus' name I pray, Amen.*

Faith

Burning Light

This morning I was reading John 12:35 which says the following: Then Jesus told them, "You are going to have the light just a little while longer. Walk while you have the light before darkness overtakes you. The man who walks in the dark does not know where he is going. Put your trust in the light while you have it so that you may become sons of light.

This verse applies to us today just as it did to His followers back then. We are to be a light shining in the darkness so that we can point others in the direction to our Lord and Savior. Just as a lighthouse shines brightly in the storm, it points the way for the ships to sail so that they will be stay safe. It is the anchor in the storm just as much as God is our anchor. So many women just go through the motion of their mundane life from laundry, the kids, the activities that overwhelm them, that they don't take time out to seek Him first to get them through from day to day. It took me 40 years of going around the mountain to realize that my light hadn't burned out completely. Once I started seeking Him daily, the passion came back, the light was ignited, and yes, I am on fire for our Lord. I want to shout it to the roof tops and spread the word so that everyone out there can know that they too have an anchor in the storms of life. It is Jesus Christ our Lord!

I heard a song this morning by Rich Mullins, "Our God is an awesome God". Not too many people know that Rich died in 1997 at the age of 41 yrs old. He was a songwriter who gave all he had to his hometown Quaker church in Indiana. Later in life, he moved to live on Navajo Reservation to share the gospel. All of his proceeds went back to his church and they gave him a minimal salary at his request. While traveling to Illinois one day to a Benefit Concert in a jeep with a friend an oncoming Tractor Trailer truck was headed for him. He swerved and was thrown from the jeep. The truck then swerved to avoid hitting the jeep after it flipped and ran right over Rich and killed him instantly. He had a light, a passion for Christ; he lived his life to the fullest to bring others to him. He gave his all. One day when my time is up, I want to know that I gave it my all and that I didn't let my light burn out. I hope my light brings others out of the darkness just as Rich Mullins did and to this day, his music still is doing just that.

So where are you today? Is your light shining brightly for others? Is it just a flicker every now and then? If it is, it's time to seek the Lord and light the way through the storms to glorify Him and bring others safely through the storm!

Prayer for today: *Father in Heaven, may my light never burn out for you and always shine brightly for others! In Jesus' name, Amen.*

Wall of Truth

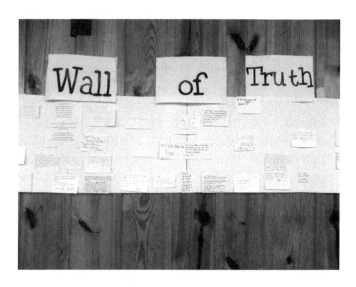

    Not too long ago I had an awesome experience at a weekend women's retreat. One of the things that stood out to me was a wall full of sayings and scripture verses that women wrote and taped on the wall. They called it the "Wall of Truth". One woman wrote, "Stay out of the Mud and the Mire." Others wrote bible passages of peace, comfort, joy, truth, etc. Today I was reminded of that wall. I am at a hospital with my son and I went out into the hallway. As I waited for the nurse to bring me a pillow from the nurse's station, the bulletin board caught my eye. It was full of cards just like the one at the retreat. Only these cards were thanking the nurses. Some read things like: thank you for showing compassion, thank you for lending a hand, thank you for showing great mercy, thank you for being so nice, thank you for just listening, thank you for praying with me, thank you for your calling. Did you know that all of those things that were said are examples of God's word and His character? When you become a Christian you take on the traits of Jesus Christ. The fruit of His Holy Spirit comes flowing naturally within you. Galatians 5:22-23 says the following "But the fruit of the Spirit is love, joy, peace, forbearance, kindness, goodness, faithfulness, gentleness and self-control. Against such things there is no law." Our Pastor says often, "You are never more like Jesus, than when Jesus is inside of you." D.L. Moody once wrote, "Character is what you are in the dark." Matthew 5:16 says "In the same way, let your light shine before men, that they may see your good deeds and praise your Father in heaven."

If we all practice being the light for Jesus to others, anyone who is walking in darkness could find their way. What wall of truth gets you by when the chips are down? Mine would be 2Timothy 1:7 "For God did not give us, the spirit of fear, but of love, power, and a sound mind."

Prayer for today: *Heavenly Father, I pray for everyone who just needs to see a flicker of Hope in you today. Father help me to be a light to those who need to feel Your presence. If someone is hurting, may You send them my way, and may You help me to be graceful and show mercy. In Jesus' name, Amen.*

Bees

Have you ever really wondered what do bees do exactly? Why did God make them with stingers that can cause tremendous pain? My mother lives in the country on 15 acres of land. She is allergic to bees. She has an epi-pen just in case she gets stung because she swells so fast that she would never make it to the hospital in time in the city. I love the movie "Fried Green Tomatoes". In the movie the character named, "Idgy", would stick her hand in a bee hive, and get fresh honey without being stung. Are you a bee charmer? I'm certainly not. A friend of mine was cutting her yard this week and she got stung. She said that her leg hurt so bad it felt like someone cut it with a machete. That's painful. Therefore, why did God make them sting? I think it was so that could protect their job. Their job is to pollinate the plants, make honey, and help break down the food chain. Bees carry the pollen from plant to plant and if they stopped doing their job, we would stop eating! They are faithful with the job they were given.

Wild bees are bees that lay up honey in Deuteronomy 32:13 and In Psalms 81:16. The honeycomb is made in hexagons. They are made in such an angle that they store the most amount of honey and use the least amount of space. Only God could create something of intelligent precision. Psalms 119:103 says the following: How sweet are thy words unto my taste! Yea sweeter than honey to my mouth. The Israelites were trying to get to the land of milk and honey. Proverbs 24:13 says the following: My son, eat thou honey, because it is good; and the honeycomb, which is sweet to thy taste. So if a bee ever stings you, just know that they are being faithful to God in doing the job he created them to and protecting it in the process. In the end, the honey will be sweet and God will be glorified. That is how we should do the job He has blessed us with so that in the end we will taste the sweetness of the honey that we produced and be blessed.

Prayer for today: *Heavenly Father, help me to see your miraculously creations in everything I see today. In Jesus' name, Amen.*

Blind but Able

Have you ever known anyone who was blind? Years ago I met a lady named Pat who was. She was born blind. She never knew what it was like to see colors and God's creations. She amazed me because at that time she seemed to be in her fifties. She lived alone in an apartment in Atlanta. She had a Seeing Eye dog that assisted her. She was a strong woman to me. It seems if you lose one of your other senses then you rely on the remainder of them. Your hearing becomes very sensitive. My heart goes out to people who are blind. I used to work for an ophthalmologist years ago, and we had some patients who had very little sight due to glaucoma or macular degeneration. It is sad to know that once you've seen God's creations and lose your sight you will never be able to experience them again. In the book of Luke 7:21 in the bible it says the following: At that very time Jesus cured many who had diseases, sicknesses and evil spirits, and gave sight to many who were blind. In the book of Matthew 15:30 it says the following: Great crowds came to him, bringing the lame, the blind, the crippled, the mute and many others, and laid them at his feet; and he healed them. Can you imagine the excitement once they could see for once in the first time in their life? I would be shouting it from the roof tops, "I'm healed"! In Matthew 20:30 it says the following: Two blind men were sitting by the roadside, and when they heard that Jesus was going by, they shouted, "Lord, Son of David, have mercy on us!" They used their sense of hearing and when they knew he was near they knew he would heal them. It took me thirty three years in my life to realize that Jesus would heal me. I wasn't blind, but I couldn't see so to speak. Until I came to know who Christ really was and grasp the concept of the cross I might as well have been blind. In the book of Acts 9:17-19 it says: Then Ananias went to the house and entered it. Placing his hands on Saul, he said, "Brother Saul, the Lord—Jesus, who appeared to you on the road as you were coming here—has sent me so that you may see again and be filled with the Holy Spirit." Immediately, something like scales fell from Saul's eyes, and he could see again. He got up and was baptized, and after taking some food, he regained his strength. Just like Saul was healed you can be healed as well. You can be out of bondage from your past and see Jesus. All you have to do is believe and call on him. You may not see him, but he sees you. In Acts 3:16 it says the following: By faith in the name of Jesus, this man whom you see and know was made strong. It is Jesus' name and the faith that comes through him that has completely healed him, as you can all see. Won't you open up your eyes and call out to him? He's closer than you think.

Prayer for today: *Heavenly Father, I pray that you would take down the scales from the eyes of the lost and that they would be able to see your love, mercy, and compassion toward them through Jesus. In His name, Amen.*

Beyond the Sunset

After it rains for several days, I need to see the sunshine. I need to feel the warmth of it on my face. If I don't see any sunshine, things start to look a little gloomy around me. I don't think I'm one of those people that could live year round in Washington State. Why do you think God created the sun?

Genesis 1:3 says the following: Then God said, "Let there be light," and there was light. He knew we would need light to guide us by day and separate it from the night time. Genesis 1:16 says the following: God made two great lights—the larger one to govern the day, and the smaller one to govern the night. He also made the stars. We need the sun for food as well. In Deuteronomy 33:14 it says the following: with the rich fruit that grows in the sun, and the rich harvest produced each month. I love to watch the sunrise at the beach. My family will stay in to sleep, but I will get up at six in the morning to get that perfect shot and spend time alone with the Lord as He greets me with a new day. I have to say that moment is one that is so special to me. I also love to watch the sunset. It's almost as if the Lord is saying, "Rest my Child, the day is over." I heard a song years ago called, "Beyond the Sunset", by Virgil Brock. He wrote it in 1936. While on Winona Lake visiting a friend, Virgil's Blind cousin spoke out with excitement and said, " What a beautiful sunset!" One of the other guests asked how it was possible for him to see events of the sky. Horace's reply was to have a lasting affect: I see through other people's eyes, and I think I often see more - I see beyond the sunset. Back at home, Virgil was inspired to write a hymn based upon the events of the evening. His

wife joined him from the piano. Horace was there also. When he heard the first three verses Horace reminded them of the storm clouds that had been hovering just above that evening's sunset, and suggested that be the theme of a fourth verse. Before the three climbed into their beds that night, Beyond the Sunset was ready for publication. Some of the lyrics go like this: Beyond the sunset, a hand will guide me, to God the Father whom I adore. His glorious presence, His words of welcome, will be my portion on that fair shore. Beyond the sunset, O glad reunion,
With our dear loved ones who've gone before, in that fair homeland we'll know no parting.
Beyond the sunset forever more. What a beautiful expression of hope in the Lord and what is waiting for us! I heard that song over twenty years ago played on the piano by my son's grandmother, Elizabeth, and it was amazing to me when I heard the words fill the room. Ever since I heard that song when I look at the sunset, I reflect on what's beyond it and what our Lord has in store.

Prayer for today: *Heavenly Father, I pray that I will always look beyond the horizon because that's where my hope is in you. In Jesus' name, Amen.*

Watch and Pray

Recently we were in a hospital chapel and there was a huge notebook where people could write down prayer request on it to God. My husband was with me and as I was checking out the beautiful Bible, he was looking at that notebook. He said, "What's this?" I told him it was like a prayer journal where you could write down your thoughts to God. He stood there and read the last persons prayer because it stood out. The handwriting was a child's. It said something to this effect, "God please help my Daddy get well. Be with him during his surgery. Don't let him die." This particular letter to God was a serious one. Only God could get that request and change things around for His glory. I don't know the outcome of that man's surgery, but I have a pretty strong feeling God heard the prayer.

Have you ever written God a letter? Before you put pen to paper, you have to think it through so it will make sense. The child who wrote the prayer for his or her dad trusted and had faith enough for God to understand what was written. It was heartfelt. It was sincere. It was a last request poured out on paper to save the life of a loved one. It was having child-like faith and believing that God would take care of the concern at hand.

Seeing the letters to God made me think of the letters Paul wrote to the churches. He wrote them with compassion for leading the lost to salvation. He not only spoke the gospel, he wrote it through faith and it was justified. In his letter to the Corinthians (1 Corinthians 4:14) he wrote, "I am writing this not to shame you but to warn you as my dear children. He cared about what happened to them." Colossians 4:2 says "Devote yourselves to prayer, being watchful and thankful." When we pray sincerely with our whole heart, we stay alert to watch and see what God does with that prayer. I don't believe we have to go to Jerusalem to write down our prayer and place it in the cracks of the Wailing Wall to be heard by God. I believe we can pray right we are with true sincerity, and God will meet us at the throne. Dr. Charles Stanley said, "Jesus encourages us to pray. He tells us to ask, seek, and knock. We ask for things, we seek understanding, and we knock on doors of opportunity that lie before us. The Lord is saying that in every area of life we can find what we are looking for by talking to the heavenly Father." Jesus set an example in the Garden of Gethsemane when he asked the disciples to watch and pray as he set out to pray himself. Matthew 26:41 says "Watch and pray so that you will not fall into temptation. The spirit is willing, but the flesh is weak."

I know that sometimes God says yes, and sometimes God says no to our prayers. Sometimes He says "Wait" because He has something better in store for you. However, we will never know what the outcome will be unless we watch and pray.

Prayer for today: *Heavenly Father, I pray that You would draw others to You who do not have a relationship with You through Jesus. Continue to wake me so I can spend time alone with You. Fill me with Your Holy Spirit, so that I can be a light to those in the darkness. Thank you for this day and all of Your blessings. Forgive me of my many sins. In Jesus' name, Amen.*

Test of Faith

Test driving a car recently was a true measure of faith. The car dealer told my husband to take his foot off the brake at 5 mph and the car would stop on its own before touching the upcoming barrels. My husband was very hesitant and slowly let off the gas pedal. When he approached the barrels he started to put his foot on the brake pedal. He chuckled a little because he knew that was a hard task. He had to have faith that the car would stop on its own. That's exactly what we do as Christians. We have faith and believe that God sent His one and only son to die on the cross for our sin debt. We have to totally have faith that God is in control.

Romans 10:17 says "Consequently, faith comes from hearing the message, and the message is heard through the word about Christ." Galatians 5:5 says "For through the Spirit we eagerly await by faith the righteousness for which we hope." Today in church we were reminded that we have never met Benjamin Franklin, and yet we believe he discovered electricity. We go to crank our car, and have faith it will crank. We go out to a restaurant and eat a perfect stranger's food, and yet we have faith we will not get sick from it. We get on an airplane and fly thousands of feet in the air, and have faith the pilot knows what he is doing. When you have an operation, you have faith the doctor knows what to do. You send your kids to school and have faith they are taken care of without you being present. Why is it so hard for people to not have faith in Jesus Christ? Hebrews 11:1 says "Now faith is confidence in what we hope for and assurance about what we do not see." The whole chapter of Hebrews 11 pretty much sums up faith for the entire bible! Rev. Franklin Graham, son of Evangelist Billy Graham, said this in a recent article "For me, the definition of a Christian is whether we have given our life to Christ and are following him in faith and we have trusted him as our lord and savior." I believe faith and trust in Jesus gives us hope in Heaven, which is security for our future. In referencing faith, Oswald Chambers wrote, "It is not even a question of the holiness of sanctification, but of something which comes much farther down the road. It is a faith that has been tried and proved and has withstood the test. Abraham is not a type or an example of the holiness of sanctification, but a type of the life of faith—a faith, tested and true, built on the true God."

Prayer for today: *Heavenly Father, I pray that You will continue to strengthen my faith in You where I am lacking so that I will not stumble. When I am tested in trials, I pray that my faith will set an example for others to be strong as well. In Jesus' name, Amen.*

Adoration

Majesty

Have you ever looked around for God's majesty in your surroundings? Webster's dictionary says the definition of majesty is greatness or splendor of quality or character. I have never been overseas to marvel at God's majesty. However, I found at times He is closer than you think.

I used to procrastinate tremendously about having to get up at 5:00 am and take our dog out. It wasn't until recently that I started looking up at the stars. I go out in my backyard before the sunrise in the mornings and just gaze at the stars that he created. Who would have thought I could look up and be so amazed by His grandeur.

There have been mornings when I would take my youngest son to school and we would look at the clouds of pink and purple. It was as if the Lord had taken a paintbrush in the sky and gave it the colors for the day. Have you ever heard that the clouds were the dust at Jesus feet?

When we go on vacation, I get up early to meet the Lord and walk the beach with Him. I am astonished at the sunrise every time and He takes my breath away.

Ever since as far back as I can remember after a rain, I look for rainbows. I love the colors in the mist and I always think of His promise to Noah. I have a friend who lost her whole family in a car accident. The day of the funeral, she looked up and there was a perfect upside down rainbow. That was her smile that she holds on to that tells her everything is going too alright. Adrian Rogers once quoted: When Jesus came the first time He came in a manager. When he comes, again He is coming in "Majesty". 1 Chronicles 29:11 says: Yours O Lord is the greatness and the power, the glory, the victory, and the majesty. Everything in the Heavens and on the earth is yours, O Lord, and this is your kingdom. We adore you and you are exalted as head over all. He my friends is coming back in Royalty robes with all His majesty for His Bride. What a glorious sight that will be! So the next time you are just in a ho hum kind of mood, all you have to do is go outside and look up and I promise you He will show you His majesty!

Prayer for today: *Heavenly Father, I pray I will always reflect on your majesty! In Jesus' name, Amen.*

T.G.I.F.

When I see the initials or hear "T.G.I.F." I always agree with whoever is saying it. Yes, Thank God it's Friday. For the most part, a lot of people have adapted that saying as a way to look forward to the weekend. Today, though, is one Friday we should be especially thankful for. Today is "Good Friday". Some of you may ask, why? Why is it such a good Friday? Today is a day of remembrance of Jesus dying on the cross and taking on all our sins.

Adoration

It's not just a good Friday, it's a great Friday because of Jesus. For the first three centuries of Christian history, every Friday was established as a day to commemorate Jesus' sacrificial death. Later in the fourth century, the Friday before Easter began to receive special status, which is why it was called "Great" Friday--as in, the greatest Friday of the church year. It was also known as Holy Friday, Long Friday and Sorrowful Friday.

For many denominations it is a day to fast, pray and take communion. One of the best books I have ever read was by Max Lucado, entitled *Six Hours One Friday*. In that book he writes "In a letter written within earshot of the sharpening blade that would sever his head, Paul urged Timothy to remember. You can almost picture the old warrior smiling as he wrote the words. 'Remember Jesus Christ, who was raised from the dead...This is the Good News I preach.' ...When times get hard, remember Jesus. When people don't listen, remember Jesus. When tears come, remember Jesus."

When disappointment is your bed partner, remember Jesus. Remember holiness in tandem with humanity. Remember the sick that were healed with callused hands. Remember the dead called from the grace with a Galilean accent. Remember the eyes of God that wept human tears. Today is more than just a "Good Friday," it is a "Hallelujah Friday"! It is a time to reflect of all that cost Christ our Savior. He took on our sin debt to proclaim freedom for the lost. John 19:30 says "When he had received the drink, Jesus said, "'It is finished.'

With that, he bowed his head and gave up his spirit."

The next time you hear "T.G.I.F." think about today being the Friday of all Fridays. The Friday Jesus gave up his life for you! 2 Timothy 2:8 says "Remember Jesus Christ, who was raised from the dead...This is the Good News!" Reflect on all the sins you have been guilty of and know that you can be forgiven because in two more days we will celebrate the resurrection of King Jesus. By His wounds and blood that was shed on this day over 2000 years ago, we are redeemed, forgiven and promised Heaven because Jesus conquered the grave and rose again!

Prayer for today: *Dear Heavenly Father, I am grateful for today. Thank you for dying on the cross and taking on my sin so I know I have been redeemed and forgiven. In Jesus' name, Amen.*

The Good News

On a recent vacation to the beach, I drew a fish in the sand. I wanted people that walked by to reflect on Jesus. I thought it would be a good way to witness. I find myself often trying to sow seeds somehow to tell others about Jesus. Our Pastor said that an evangelical Christian can't keep the gospel inside. They have to tell the good news! Sometimes I think that of myself. It's hard to keep quiet. It is said that during the persecution of the early church, a Christian meeting someone new would draw a

single arc in the sand. If the other person was a Christian, he or she would complete the drawing of a fish with a second arc. If the second person was not a Christian, the ambiguity of the half-symbol would not reveal the first person as a Christian. Back then you had to keep things quiet about Christ, due to persecution. I live in the United States and am grateful for the freedom of religion we have so we can worship God. There are countries today that imprison and even kill those found practicing Christianity. It is Easter and I can't imagine being in another country and not being able to say out loud, "He is Risen!" I pray for our missionaries around the world. Isaiah 53:5 says "But he was pierced for our transgressions, he was crushed for our iniquities; the punishment that brought us peace was on him, and by his wounds we are healed." Proverbs 25:25 says "As cold waters to a thirsty soul, so is good news from a far country." Charles

Spurgeon once wrote in reference to that verse "First, good news from God for sinners is like cold waters to a thirsty soul. Secondly, good news from heaven for saints is like cold waters to a thirsty soul. And, thirdly, good news in heaven from earth—the good news which reaches that far country, every now and then,—is to angels and glorified Saints as cold waters to a thirsty soul."

We are to proclaim the good news of Jesus Christ's resurrection. We are to reach the nations. Today Christians are celebrating the fact that the tomb was empty. That's the good news, and I hope that if you are reading this and you don't have a relationship with Jesus that carries you all year long that you will come to know Christ today! He is waiting. All you have to do is believe. Romans 5:10 says "For if, while we were God's enemies, we were reconciled to him through the death of his Son, how much more, having been reconciled, shall we be saved through his life." John 3:16 says "For God so loved the world that he gave his one and only Son, that whoever believes in him shall not perish but have eternal life."

Good news from God is found in Jesus dying on the cross for our sins and rising again to overcome Satan. Won't you glorify God today by believing in Jesus today, so you can share the good news with others as well? Good news is great news when it involves the grace God gave us in sending Jesus to conquer the grave!

Prayer for today: *Heavenly Father, I pray that the millions of people all over the world will be drawn to You today as they hear the message of the good news that Jesus is Risen. I pray for those that are lost and need a relationship with You will realize Jesus paid their sin debt by dying on the cross so they wouldn't have to. For I ask in Jesus' name, Amen.*

Miracle Birth

Have you ever wondered about the miracle of a child being born? I had a doctor tell me once that miracles were few and far between. Hello, red flag! God makes his miracles known to us every day of the year. Sometimes, we don't have look very far. All we have to do is look into the eyes of children. This week, my niece delivered a new baby girl into this world. She knew and planned for her to be born this week. She was prepared. She now has a child like no other. That is her family's miracle. Now she will love and nurture that baby and grow her up in the way God has instructed her. Mary truly got to witness a miracle growing inside of her. Once she got the news she was going to deliver the son of God, she immediately had a very tall order to fill. Jesus was born in a lowly stable which was the essence of humility. Mary and Joseph didn't put their baby up for adoption. They chose to feed and nurture their newborn as God instructed. Jesus was their miracle. In actuality we all are miracles once we become followers of Jesus. When we become "born again" we are a new creature in Christ. In John 3:3, it says the following: Jesus answered and said unto him, Verily, verily, I say unto thee, Except a man be born again, he cannot see the kingdom of God. We no longer put on our old self, but have a new self. We begin to see our purpose in life and start living for the one who gave us life. In Romans 6:6-7 it says the following: For we know that our old self was crucified with him so that the body ruled by sin might be done away with, that we should no longer be slaves to sin because anyone who has died has been free from sin. The new birth is that we are "born again"! I am so thankful I have a new self and buried my old self. You can have that new birth in your life. If you've never had the experience of witnessing the birth of a child, a caterpillar changing to a butterfly, a bee making honey, there is another way to experience a miracle. It's accepting Jesus Christ as your personal Lord and Savior and asking him into your life. Once you do, you will experience your life changing. You will no longer have worldly desires, but will have the desires in your heart that brings God glory. That's why he created us. To bring Him glory. In Romans 12:2, it says the following: Do not conform to the pattern of this world, but be transformed by the renewing of your mind. Then you will be able to test and approve what God's will is—his good, pleasing and perfect will. He changed my life, he changed my mind. He made me a "New Dawn", and that is my miracle.

Prayer for today: *Heavenly Father, I thank you for continually molding me into the new creation you have called me to be. Sharpen my mind and stamp your word in it and on my heart so that I will continue to grow in you. In Jesus' name, Amen.*

A Father's Love

Today is Fathers Day and I am reflecting this morning on my dad of course, but also on my heavenly father. I remember being in the garden with my dad as a little girl, and he was teaching me how to hoe out the weeds. I must have been six years old. While I was walking behind him, a garden snake came in between us. Immediately, he turned around with the hoe and killed the snake as I stood there and screamed. He protected me. Thinking of protection, I had to also reflect on our heavenly father who watches over us. In Psalms 5:11 it says "But let all who take refuge in you be glad; let them ever sing for joy. Spread your protection over them, that those who love your name may rejoice in you."

Our Heavenly father watches over us! Psalms 68:4 says "Sing to God, sing in praise of his name, extol him who rides on the clouds; rejoice before him—his name is the LORD. A father to the fatherless, a defender of widows, is God in his holy dwelling." I am also reminded of a song called "Lead Me" by Sanctus Real. In that song the wife is praying for the husband to be the man she's longed for, to stand up and be strong when she can't, to fight and to be the father he was called to be to their children. The latter part of the song is the man is praying to God to show him the way to do just those

Adoration

things.

I believe being a good father requires wisdom, discernment, love, patience and the characteristics of Jesus Christ. My dad protected me when I was little that day by thinking quickly, and yes, that probably didn't require much. However, I as a child was in fear and he was there to watch over me.

If your father has passed on or you don't have a close relationship with him, I pray that you will lean on your Heavenly Father today. He loves you, He protects you, He sent his son to die for you. In his book, *What a Son Needs From His Dad: How a Man Prepares His Sons For Life*, author Dr. Michael O'Donnell says, "We've got to be there for our sons. The world is impacting them and calling to them all the time. The day they leave home will be the moment of truth. Will they be ready to stand on their own two feet? Will they have sufficient moral courage to do what is right?" A father's love is something we all desire, cherish and will remember. Today on Father's day, I hope you will do just that.

Prayer for today: *Heavenly Father, I thank you for demonstrating how we are to love, how You loved us more than anyone or anything and how to lean on You to learn what it means to be a great parent when we do not know how. In Jesus' name, Amen.*

Leaving a Legacy

I recently visited my mom in South Georgia. One morning I had to go down to Bob's Country Store. When I did the cashier asked who I was and when I told her whose daughter I was, she immediately told me great things about my mother. She told me how well respected she was in the community. She told me that my mother would do anything for anybody and would go out of her way in the process. She introduced me to everyone in the store as Carroll's daughter. The same day while at my mom's antique shop I met the owner next door. When he realized whose daughter I was, he immediately told me I had "fine" parents. I felt honored. I felt privileged. Tonight back in my home town I attended a dinner party. The hostess had her mom attending. She also had her children serving. At the end of the dinner, her mother said wonderful things of her daughter, Angie. I couldn't help but notice how beautiful she was. I noticed not only was she proud of Angie but of her grandchildren as well. Look at the legacy she is passing down. What are you doing for your children? Are you leaving a legacy for them to follow that will glorify God? Did you know that we are daughters of the King? In Ephesians 1:5, it says the following: "He predestined us to be adopted as his sons through Jesus Christ, in accordance with his pleasure and will." In Galatians 3:28-29 it says the following: There is neither Jew nor Greek, slave nor free, male nor female, for you are all one in Christ Jesus. If you belong to Christ, then you are Abraham's seed, and heirs according to the promise." In Romans 8:17 it says: Now if we are children, then we are heirs—heirs of God and co-heirs with Christ, if indeed we share in his sufferings in order that we may also share in his glory." In 1 Peter, 2:9 it says the following: "You are a chosen people, a royal priesthood, a holy nation, a people belonging to God, that you may declare the praises of him who called you out of darkness into his wonderful light". We are set apart. We are a chosen people. We were purchased for a purpose and were consecrated by God for his possession. There is a song by Nicole Nordeman called "Legacy". Some of the lyrics are as follows: I want to leave a legacy. How will they remember me? Did I choose to love? Did I point to you enough to make a mark on things? God has already left us an inheritance through his son, Jesus. Once you become a believer, you are adopted in to the family of God. It gives me great joy to know I am a daughter of the King. I want my children to see Him in me as well as others. I want to leave a legacy. Don't you?

Prayer for today: *Heavenly Father, I pray that I will always set a good example in front of my children so that they can be a light in the darkness. Help me to be show the fruits of your spirit daily in their presence and be a good role model. In Jesus' name, Amen.*

Discouragement

Daily Task

When thinking of what I have to do today and get done before sunset sometimes I wonder, "Will I get it all done?" Each of us have different task from things as simple as laundry & the dishes to big suit meetings & presentations. I can't imagine now how I used to get through my day in years past. I now seek the Lord first before the sun rise to help me with my schedule that lay ahead of me. My house is not white glove clean, but it flows and functions to the best of my ability for that given day so I don't stress over it.

When looking at Moses in the Old testament I have to think he was little overwhelmed from time to time. He had fear, he had doubts, he was discouraged, and he was tired. God still used him to lead the people out of bondage. If Moses looked at his task and gave up just at thought of his daily schedule that was awaiting him then he wouldn't have fulfilled Gods plan.

There is a song by Ernie Haas that says, "My God will send a Moses to lead you out". Sometimes if you are not the one to help someone in need then God will send someone to help you if you are the one carrying the burden. Learn to pray and trust Him to see you through whatever you are worried about. You never know you just might be sitting at the edge of the Promised Land the whole time and have no idea how close you are to the milk and

47

honey! Matthew 11:30 says the following: For my yolk is easy and my burden is light. Christ carried our burdens when he carried the cross. He then put them to rest when he died for us. No matter what you have ahead of you bring it to the cross. He will see you through your day.

Prayer for today: *Heavenly Father, Please help me stay focused on the task you have laid before me this day. In Jesus' name, Amen.*

Closet Clutter

Yesterday, as I was cleaning I noticed how much over the Christmas Holidays I just crammed things into my closet. I couldn't see the floor and normally that is my place to get away from everyone and spend time with God and pray. Christmas paper, bags, clothes, purses, shoes, were all stacked and piled up galore. It made me think, what if Jesus knocked on my door and said, "Dawn, let's go pray"? I would be so embarrassed, as I should be. I need to get organized for this new year and plan on doing that today. So, how clean is your closet? The bible says in the book of Matthew 12:44 the following: Then it says, 'I will return to the house I left.' When it arrives, it finds the house unoccupied, swept clean and put in order. Jesus was using a parable here and telling that once one demon leaves you and you get yourself in order if the demon can't find anyone to corrupt he will come back to that same person with seven demons. That tells me you better have your armor on and be kept pure and clean. Right now my closet is nothing but clean. If I looked at myself as a closet so the demons are not piling up, I would tell you I am in need of constant prayer. I have to pray daily for God to cleanse me of any unrighteousness and impurities. Thoughts from the enemy can come in and take up residence if you allow it to happen. Romans 12:2 says the following: Do not conform to the pattern of this world, but be transformed by the renewing of your mind. Then you will be able to test and approve what God's will is—his good, pleasing and perfect will. In order to transform your mind, you have to fill it and sharpen it daily with God's word. Warren Weirsbe once wrote: For worship is the submission of all our nature to God. It is the quickening of conscience by His holiness; the nourishment of "mind" with His truth; the purifying of imagination by His beauty; the opening of the heart to His love; the surrender of will to His purpose -- and all of this gathered up in adoration, the most selfless emotion of which our nature is capable and therefore the chief remedy for that self-centeredness which is our original sin and the source of all actual sin. We have to constantly feed our mind to stand against the enemy so that he doesn't come in our life and clutter up our minds. If he the enemy is allowed to come in and take up residence, the clutter will start to pile up and Jesus will not have any room. I don't know about your prayer closet or even if you have a place to spend time alone with the Lord, but if you do make it one that says: Lord, come on in and have a seat with me and let's spend some time together.

Prayer for today: *Heavenly Father, I pray that you would give me the strength to get done all the task I need to accomplish today. Help me with my home and getting organized. If the enemy comes, I want him to know he is walking on Holy ground. Thank you for keeping me on track with your will in my life. In Jesus' name, Amen.*

My GPS

While driving to a doctor appointment today I was totally lost. I had punched into my GPS system the address and due to a major accident, I was re-routed to an alternate route. There was another delay and then I was rerouted again. At one point, I missed my turn and could feel my hands clinching the wheel. I was on a time schedule and had less than thirty minutes to get there. I heard the words recalculating and before you knew it, I arrived at my destination. Isn't that usually the way God is steering us in the right direction. If we seek him first, listen to his instruction, we will arrive at the destination he has intended for us to be on. I think of the Israelites often and how they went around the mountain for forty years. They had the instructions; however, they chose to do things their own way Instead of listening to God. If they had only listened to him, first they could have enjoyed the promise land a whole lot sooner and avoided a lot of heartache. I know someone who has been married several times. She knows God and is a believer. She stays on the right road with him for a while and then all of the sudden she takes a detour off the map. How does that happen? She has the instruction manual which is God's word and she doesn't listen to what he is telling her. When he says recalculating, you better listen. Otherwise, you just might end up going around that same mountain and never know what God has in store for you. She thinks she is in control and that is why she continues to make the same mistakes repeatedly. Psalms 23:3 says: he refreshes my soul. He guides me along the right paths for his name's sake. Psalms 48:18 says the following: For this God is our God forever and ever, he will be our guide even to the end. All we have to do is let God be our Guide and we will stay on the right path through life's trials. The next time you think that you need your GPS try seeking "God's Pathway System" and He will be your guide. We may not have a pillar cloud in front of us to lead us out of the wilderness but we do have Gods word.

Prayer for today: *Heavenly Father, may you always guide my steps and walk before me and behind me. Help me to not waiver to the left or right but stay on target right where you want me to be. In Jesus' name, Amen.*

51

When it Rains it Pours

My mom always has told me for years, "Don't get out your umbrella until it starts to rain". What she means is not to worry more than you have to. I had a friend tell me once if Noah waited on the rain to pull out his umbrella he would have been in a mess. Great point! It's all about being prepared. God sends the rain when we need it. It's up to us to receive it and weather the storm to the best of our ability. There are a lot of trials in this life. I have gone through many. I have lost loved ones; been through divorce, lost jobs, just to name a few. The one that is the hardest for me is taking care of my son who has a life threatening illness. It's a constant up and down journey. Sometimes it just mists rain. Sometimes it storms. Sometimes it hails. Sometimes we get to see the rainbow. My son had to have a liver transplant at age four. He is now sixteen. He is doing well for the moment. He has been through blood transfusions, rejection, and several viruses. He also has played baseball, tee ball in elementary school and junior varsity in high school. Looking on the outside, you would never know anything was wrong. Sometimes though on the inside, the doctors tell us things aren't what they should be. He takes medications. He has blood work often. We do what the doctors say and ride out the storm. I used to worry and fret. It took several years not to do that. Now, I just praise God for every day he's given me with my son and we just keep pressing on. In Leviticus 26:4 it says: I will send you rain in its season, and the ground will

Discouragement

yield its crops and the trees their fruit. Without the rain, there would be no harvest. Without the rain, there would be no joy. We have to have the rain in our lives so that we can praise God for the sunshine when the storm is over. Matthew 7:25 says:

The rain came down, the streams rose, and the winds blew and beat against that house; yet it did not fall, because it had its foundation on the rock. Although it continues to rain on us through trials and tribulations while we are here on this earth, God is our shelter in the storm. If you have Jesus as your foundation, you can weather any storm that may come your way. He is the cornerstone. All you have to do is be prepared for the storm that's going to come at some point in your life when you least expect it. Put on your shield, hold on to your faith, and trust in the Lord to see you through it.

Prayer for Today: *Heavenly Father, I pray today that you would always remind me that you are my anchor through the storms and that you are with me to ride out the storm no matter what may come my way! In Jesus' name, Amen.*

Fear

Being Afraid

Some people are in fear of a lot more than others. It could be anything from heights, to darkness, to even small spiders. I recently started thinking about other people's fears and not so much the focus on mine. My youngest son has to have his nightlight on for fear of the dark. I have to admit things look a whole lot better in the light that's for sure! I have never really noticed my oldest son scared of anything much until recently. He is 16 years old. He is muscular from lifting weights and he pretty much brags about being stronger than me with a smile of course. Well, this past week I was downstairs. He came running downstairs with his cousin who is 16 as well and they both were screaming for me. I thought what in the world is going on. Turns out, I had to kill a hornet that had come into his room through the cracked window. Now I know my son has a whole lot of strength but when it comes to bees, spiders, and snakes, he turns into a little boy again in an instant. I have never laughed so hard at the two of them this past week. In addition, my husband went out in the kayak and as he was on the lake, a black snake swam underneath his boat. He immediately held his legs way up in the air and was frightened. It is fear! Where does it come from? To the woman who has a fear of being attacked and is tormented with it for years it's a scary thing. To the man who is in fear of losing his job. To the woman who just lost her husband and doesn't know how she's going to make ends meet. To the family whose home was just foreclosed on. To the child who was just diagnosed with a life threatening illness. Again, it is fear. I have heard that the word "fear" is mentioned in the bible 366 times. That is a bible verse every day including leap year so that you cannot forget that God says to Fear not! My sister told me several years ago about the verse 2 Timothy 1:7. It says the following: For God did not give us a spirit of fear, but of power, of love, and of a sound mind. Did you hear that? If He didn't give it to us then where in the world is it coming from? Satan! He puts fear in our minds of the unknown when we don't trust in Almighty God. We see it on television through the media and it becomes part of our children's minds. We hear it in listening to the wrong music. I can find a whole lot of depression in one country song to last a whole year! My greatest fear I think would be to lose my family. I would go through all of the emotions of fear, anxiety, anger, depression, uncertainty, and sadness. However, in the end God would pick me up, stand me back on my feet, and encourage me to be a light to those who are going through the same thing. I am trusting in my Savior. Are you?

Prayer for today: *Heavenly Father, Please continue to remind me that fear comes from the enemy. There is no fear in you for your said, "Fear Not". Thank you Father for your constant protection over my family. In Jesus' name, Amen.*

No Fear

While on vacation at the beach, we've seen young children surfing and boogie boarding with very little supervision. They act like they don't have a worry in the world. We've also passed many people riding motorcycles without helmets. I looked up the South Carolina law and it is only required for age twenty-one and younger. Two things come to mind. The parable about the little children coming to Jesus with child-like faith like He wants us to do comes to mind. The other thing is putting on your helmet of salvation in Ephesians chapter 6.

These two different groups of people shared something in common – "No Fear. "   The little children under age ten surfing definitely had no fear of sharks nor did they seem to fear the water! The men riding without their helmets had no fear of ever getting involved in an accident. How can we go through life without having fear? How can we be sure of ourselves, without a doubt? Webster's dictionary states that the definition of fear is "to be afraid, expect with alarm."

The word "fear" is mentioned over 300 times throughout the Bible. Sometimes it is used as a reference of being in awe of God. Other times it is about being afraid. The bible says to "fear not" 366 times. That's a verse for every day of the year including leap year! In 2 Timothy 1:7 it says "For the Spirit God gave us does not make us timid, but gives us power, love and self-discipline." If God doesn't give it to us, then you know it comes from Satan! That verse tells me that when I am afraid, I need to tell Satan to flee by the authority of Jesus! James 4:7 says "Submit yourselves, then, to God. Resist the devil, and he will flee from you." And Isaiah 35:4 says "Say to those with fearful hearts, 'Be strong, do not fear; your God will come, he will come with vengeance; with divine retribution he will come to save you.'" We have to trust that our God is watching over us, trust that He will provide, protect us and have faith that He can move a mountain!

Adrian Rogers once wrote, "Worry is the noxious first cousin to fear. Fear and worry will do to you what grit does to machinery — shut you down. But God gives us the victory with His power, His love, and the gift of a sound mind. The Holy Spirit is your Bodyguard. He walks with you. The man who can kneel before God can stand before any man."

If Jesus is walking with you, and God has you in His right hand, then Satan cannot make you stumble! Walk in peace knowing that today!

Prayer for today: *Heavenly Father, I pray that by putting on my helmet of salvation I am always reminded of the victory I have over Satan and his lies! I pray that others will learn to trust in You and no matter what happens to our earthen vessels, we will hold on to the hope in Heaven we have found through Your son, Jesus. In Jesus' name, Amen.*

Standing without Slipping

Leaving church yesterday, we decided to walk down a stairway outside. I was holding my son's hand and he slipped and almost fell backwards and on his bottom. Luckily I was able to save him from the fall. There was water on the steps and we didn't see it. Immediately it made me think of how Satan is waiting to trip us up and make us fall! In the book of Psalms chapter 73:2 it says this, "But as for me, my feet had almost slipped; I had nearly lost my foothold."

Have you ever been tempted to do something you knew was not right and almost did it? If you ever used to drink alcohol or smoke, Satan will surely try and trip you up by surrounding you with people who do or through the media to make you crave it. He will do the same with food or whatever your weakness is. If you have repented of that sin then you have to stand guard and be ready. In the book of Ephesians it says to not let the devil get a foothold. Well, how do we do that you may ask? Ephesians 6:10-17 says "Finally, be strong in the Lord and in his mighty power. Put on the full armor of God, so that you can take your stand against the devil's schemes. For our struggle is not against flesh and blood, but against the rulers, against the authorities, against the powers of this dark world and against the spiritual forces of evil in the heavenly realms. Therefore put on the full armor of God, so that when the day of evil comes, you may be able to stand your ground, and after you have done everything, to stand. Stand firm then, with the belt of truth buckled around your waist, with the breastplate of righteousness in place, and with your feet fitted with the readiness that comes from the gospel of peace. In addition to all this, take up the shield of faith, with which you can extinguish all the flaming arrows of the evil one. Take the helmet of salvation and the sword of the Spirit, which is the word of God." We must put on this armor daily to fight the devil and his demons! The spirit world is full of spiritual warfare. Satan is in the atmosphere and will most certainly overtake your mind if you allow him to. He will give you doubts, discouragement and throw you into a depression in a minute unless you stand guard. One little word has the authority over Satan, his demons and his battle against us. That word is "Jesus"! He gave us the authority to shut Satan down by giving us His Holy Spirit. It's time we take a stand as the church and teach that we have that authority, take up our armor and stand on the solid rock of certainty!

Prayer for today: *Heavenly Father, I pray that You will help me to stay strong in Your word. Sharpen my mind with Your word to fight off the enemy. Fill me with Your Holy Spirit to overflowing and teach me to be bold enough to know that I have the power in me to win this battle! In Jesus' name, Amen.*

Ready for War

This past week my dad and I went on a picnic by the river. As we sat there we met an older gentleman with a WWII Vet hat on who was fishing. His name was John. He was 87 years old. He served in the Army under General Patton in his "Third Army" 17th Airborne Division. He enlisted at the young age of only 16 years old. He said that he never thought he would live to be 21! He was in the Army 6 years, 3 months and 5 days. He was married for 51 years before his wife went to be with the Lord in 2002. I really enjoyed listening to his story. What intrigued me the most was that he told me how he accepted Christ at a young age, but Satan had his way and pulled him back into a life of sin. Later in life he rededicated to Christ alongside his wife and is now ready to meet Jesus. Praise! Listening to his story made me think of the battles that he overcame throughout his life. Wounded, but yet still alive and well. God is good. It made me think of being ready for battle. Are we ready?

Our own mind is a battlefield that Satan loves to try and manipulate, tempt and confuse. One thing for sure is that God is not the author of confusion. 2 Timothy 1:7 says "For the Spirit God gave us does not make us timid, but gives us power, love and a sound mind." The Forerunner Commentary says about this verse "The concept of a 'sound mind' has more to do with our attitude than we may realize. If our mind is sound, it is not cluttered up with the cares of this world. Its processes start with God and end with God. It recognizes the power of God and His love for us. However, having and maintaining a sound mind requires constant work, a positive approach, and an acceptance of both the good and the bad. It needs continual stirring, like a simmering pot on the stove. We have to guard it and exercise it at all times." Philippians 4:7 says "And the peace of God, which transcends all understanding, will guard your hearts and your minds in Christ Jesus." If we are walking in peace with God, we've got our Army boots on! Ephesians 6:14-17 says "Stand firm then, with the belt of truth buckled around your waist, with the breastplate of righteousness in place, and with your feet fitted with the readiness that comes from the gospel of peace. In addition to all this, take up the shield of faith, with which you can extinguish all the flaming arrows of the evil one. Take the helmet of salvation and the sword of the Spirit, which is the word of God."

I don't know about you, but I've got my Army boots on and they are laced up tight. I am walking in peace and ready for war and I hope you are too!

Prayer for today: *Heavenly Father, help me win this battle against Satan that's ahead of me. Walk with me daily. Send Your guardian angels to go ahead oh me and also be my rear guard. Keep me strong in Faith in knowing that You are in control and with You there is no fear, anxiety, or worry. Thank you Father for Your many blessings. I praise Your almighty name. For You are worthy. In Jesus' name, Amen.*

The Right Room

This past weekend I had the awesome pleasure of serving at a Women's Retreat. It was in a lodge by a lake with dorm style rooms and bunk beds. After we unpacked and got settled in our room, my girlfriend and I decided to go downstairs and set up our product table. After meeting with everyone and attending a concert that night, we went back upstairs to our room to settle in. As I walked in I noticed a cell phone that was not mine was beside my bed. I asked my friend if it was hers, and she said no. Then all of a sudden a lady came in and looked dumbfounded. She said she had unpacked all of her things in our room, but it was obviously the wrong room. She quickly got her belongings and set out for another room.

The next night during our discussion time I wound up at the same table with the same woman. After teaching, worship and testimony she came to me and took me by the hands and cried. She shared her testimony with me and it was very similar to mine. She had harbored her testimony inside of her for twenty-four years and finally was able to overcome Satan and release the weight of the bondage she was carrying! As I reflected back on her, it dawned on me that the Holy Spirit had been leading her to me when we first got there, and she had no idea. Luke 4:1 says "Jesus, full of the Holy Spirit, left the Jordan and was led by the Spirit into the wilderness." In John Chapter 4 the scripture talks of Jesus meeting the Samaritan woman at the well. He went out of his way to meet her and free her up. It was on His agenda. He knew she would be tired from her journey and she needed living water that only he could give. Charles Spurgeon once wrote "Souls have to be brought to salvation by a gentleness and wisdom such as the Savior used when He fascinated the Samaritan woman into eternal life and enticed her to the truth."

For whatever reason God used me as a vessel to overcome this lady's bondage. After she heard my testimony and realized it was the same as hers, the Holy Spirit moved her and *Satan didn't have a chance*. Revelation 12:11 says "They triumphed over him by the blood of the Lamb and by the word of their testimony; they did not love their lives so much as to shrink from death." I honestly feel she was in the "Right Room" the entire time!

Prayer for today: *Heavenly Father may You always open my eyes to see, ears to hear and heart to listen to be able to share the gospel of Your wondrous love with whomever You place in my room and my surroundings. In Jesus' name, Amen.*

Keeping it Hidden

Yesterday, I was cleaning up our play room. I looked over and beside the television tucked behind the Lincoln logs case, next to the hot wheels case was a pile of trash! I found wrappers, empty juice boxes, and even empty Gatorade bottles. Both of my boys were using that area as their trash can and was certain I would never find out. Wrong again!

It was the same last week when I discovered a not so nice texting conversation on my teenagers cell phone. He put a password on his phone, thinking that good ole mom is not smart enough to figure I out. Wrong again! Isn't it this way sometimes when we sin? We know we are doing wrong, but if we keep it hidden no one will find out. Well, let's see what God's word says? Matthew 10:26 says the following: "So do not be afraid of them, for there is nothing concealed that will not be disclosed, or hidden that will not be made known.

It repeats again in Mark 4:22 it says the same: For whatever is hidden is meant to be disclosed, and whatever is concealed is meant to be brought out into the open. Also in Luke 8:17 again it says: For there is nothing hidden that will not be disclosed, and nothing concealed that will not be known or brought out into the open. God revealed with Adam and Eve their sin to them in the beginning. He knew what King David's sin was, when he sent Nathan to tell him, "You are that man"! God knew David's sin way before David sinned. Charles Spurgeon did a sermon on hidden sin once. He wrote: There is no hiding it from God. Thy sin is photographed in high heaven; the deed when it was done was photographed upon the sky, and there it shall remain, and thou shalt see thyself one day revealed to the gazing eyes of all men, a hypocrite, a pretender, who didst sin in fancied secret, observed in all thine acts by the all-seeing Jehovah. O what fools men are, to think they can do anything in secret. God is all knowing and we can't run from God! When I sin God brings it to light immediately and I am asking forgiveness on my knees. Sometimes though I have to pray and ask God to reveal where I have sinned. If I wait long enough to listen, He tells me. 1 Corinthians 4:5 says this: Therefore judge nothing before the appointed time; wait until the Lord comes. He will bring to light what is hidden in darkness and will expose the motives of the heart. At that time each will receive their praise from God. God is the light in the darkness, and darkness can't stand the light. If there is sin to be hidden, it won't stay hidden long!

Prayer for today: *Heavenly Father please cleanse my heart of all unrighteousness. Where there is sin, bring it to the surface and reveal it to me so that I will become aware of it and ask forgiveness. In Jesus' name, Amen.*

Fear

Security

Secure Foundation

Recently I have had two different neighbors come to me with devastating news about their spouse's health. The diagnosis in both cases is a tumor. The look on their faces, is one of worry, anxiety, and uncertainty. They asked me to pray for them. Immediately, we prayed together right then. Going through a crisis is never easy. When my son needed a liver transplant years ago, I didn't seek the Lord to get me through the trying time. It was such a heavy weight and would have been a lot lighter had I had a relationship with Jesus. In the Bible, in Matthew 11:28 it says the following: Come to me, all you who are weary and burdened, and I will give you rest. Eleven years ago, I knew to go to him, but didn't seek Him wholeheartedly. Having a secure foundation is just like owning a house on the coast. You better make sure your foundation is secure because when a hurricane comes it's got to be able to stand. Did you know the Bible talks of Jesus as the cornerstone? In Mark 12:10 it says the following: Haven't you read this passage of Scripture: "'The stone the builders rejected has become the cornerstone. In Acts 4:11 it says the following: Jesus is "'the stone you builders rejected, which has become the cornerstone.' Without Jesus as your cornerstone, your house is going to crumble under pressure. Satan will look for ways to enter your house. You have to make sure that it is secure. If our body is where Jesus resides, then we need to ask God to make sure it's constantly cleansed from all unrighteousness. How are your heart, soul, mind, and strength lately? In Luke 10:27 it says the following: He answered, "'Love the Lord your God with all your heart and with all your soul and with all your strength and with all your mind'; and, 'Love your neighbor as yourself.' "This is the greatest commandment. I will definitely be in prayer for my neighbors and their trials that they are going through. I hope that their foundation is secure to withstand the trial. In Matthew 7:26 it says the following: But, everyone who hears these words of mine and does not put them into practice is like a foolish man who built his house on sand. Is Jesus your cornerstone? Is he your foundation so that you can weather the storm? If you're not prepared, the wind, rain, and hail, will come and you will not be able to stand.

Prayer for today: *Heavenly Father, I pray that I will always be grounded in you and that my foundation will not crumble. In Jesus' name, Amen.*

Our Insurance Policy

Today while driving, I ran across a billboard sign. It was an advertisement for an insurance company. It said, "We will protect you through Fire, Storms, and Water." It made me think of the protection we have with God through His son, Jesus. He is our insurance policy for eternal life. In

Security

the book of proverbs 2:8 it says the following: for he guards the course of the just and protects the way of his faithful ones. In the book of Isaiah 43:2 it says: When you pass through the waters, I will be with you; and when you pass through the rivers, they will not sweep over you. When you walk through the fire, you will not be burned; the flames will not set you ablaze. His word reminds me often that through the trials of this life God watches over us day in and day out. Will there be fire and storms? Yes, however, when we go through those trials He will pick us up and put us right back on our feet and we will look back and be stronger than we were before. Whenever the blows of this life come at you in all directions and you feel overwhelmed, anxious, uncertain about the future please know that God will never leave you nor forsake you. It says in the book of Deuteronomy 31:8 The LORD himself goes before you and will be with you; he will never leave you nor forsake you. Do not be afraid; do not be discouraged." In the book of Matthew 6:34 Therefore do not worry about tomorrow, for tomorrow will worry about itself. Each day has enough trouble of its own. We are to stay focused on the day given to us and make the most of it as living for our God in everything we do. If we did that, we wouldn't have time to worry about tomorrow. Do you have a spiritual insurance policy for yourself? Do you know that through Jesus Christ all things are possible? Or, does your policy need to be renewed? In the book of Philippians 4:6 it says: Do not be anxious about anything, but in every situation, by prayer and petition, with thanksgiving, present your requests to God. God has given you Jesus Christ, his one and only son as your insurance policy to get through the trials of this life and know how to have life eternal with Him in Heaven. All you have to do is get out His policy called," His Word" and accept His son Jesus as your personal Lord and Savior. Ask Him to forgive you of your sins and be the Lord of your life and He will write your name in the Lambs Book of Life. You will then have His Holy Spirit to help you and live inside you. Your policy with God will be rock solid and never expire!

Prayer for Today: *Heavenly Father, I thank you for reminding me that you are my security throughout this life and without you I have nothing. In Jesus' name, Amen.*

Covenant Property

Yesterday I went out walking, and as I got to the front of our subdivision I noticed a little sign that read, "Covenant Property Protected Community". I have passed it dozens of times, but never really paid that much attention to it. So my mind started turning and focusing on the word covenant. To me that word means commitment. Webster's Dictionary defines covenant as this: a mutual agreement of two or more persons or parties, or one of the stipulations in such an agreement.

Biblically, according to Wordnet, the definition for covenant would be the following: an agreement between God and his people in which God makes certain promises and requires certain behavior from them in return. The word covenant is mentioned close to 300 times in the bible. Are we all in agreement with God, just as we are in our Home Owners Association? The old covenant before Christ between God and His people was to serve God and you will be rewarded. Genesis 9:9 says "I now establish my covenant with you and with your descendants after you." God was making a promise to Noah that He would never destroy the entire earth again by flood. Genesis 17:2 says that God made a covenant with Abraham: "Then I will make my covenant between me and you and will greatly increase your numbers." He later shared His covenant with Moses when God etched His Commandments on stone for the people to abide by. Exodus 16:34 says, "As the LORD commanded Moses, Aaron put the manna with the tablets of the covenant law, so that it might be preserved." The New Covenant is the price Jesus paid for all of us at the Cross. Luke 22:20 says "In the same way, after the supper he took the cup, saying, 'This cup is the new covenant in my blood, which is poured out for you.'"

When you accept God's son Jesus as your personal Lord and Savior, you are in agreement that He died on the cross for you so that you will not go to hell. You are in agreement that you need to repent from living a sinful life, change your worldly ways and live for Christ alone. You don't sign a dotted line with a thousand papers, but you simply ask Jesus to be the Lord of your life and take control of it and He does. His Holy Spirit then comes into your very heart and soul, which instills His character inside you. Then and only then will you exemplify the ways of Christ such as love, joy, peace, gentleness, kindness, forbearance, goodness, self-control and faithfulness. When speaking of Jesus, Charles Spurgeon once wrote, "We commence then by the first thing, which is enough to startle us by its immense value; in fact, unless it had been written in God's Word, we never could have dreamed that such a blessing could have been ours. God himself, by the covenant becomes the believer's own portion and inheritance. 'I will be their God.'" I now look at the term "covenant" totally differently in my life and I hope you will too. Through Jesus the covenant was restored where it was once broken.

Prayer for today: *Heavenly Father, I thank you for sending Jesus through Your grace and mercy to save me from myself. Forgive me of my sins. Help me to be the follower of Christ and walk the path you desire for me to walk so that you will delight in me as I delight in You. In Jesus' name I pray, Amen.*

Birds Singing

Over the weekend, I got up early to take out our dog. It had to only be around 5:00 a.m. The stars were still out and I could see the moon. What caught my attention was the sound of baby birds. They were singing, and chirping. I could picture in my mind how hungry they were and waiting for their mother's return with their breakfast. In Luke 12:6, it says the following: Are not 5 sparrows sold for two pennies. Yet God forgets not one of them. He watches over even the tiniest bird and feeds them. So what are you worried about? If we focus on our protection, our property, or worrying about tomorrow do we not fully trust in God? He watches over us. He provides for us. He protects us. Matthew 6:26 says the following: Look at the birds of the air; they do not sow, reap, or store away in barns, and yet your heavenly Father feeds them. Are you not much more valuable than they? Do you trust in Him to provide for you? Have you turned over to Him the crisis that you just can't seem to get through? Are you putting your faith in the one that heals? Are you relying on Him enough to wait on His reply before you make that important decision?

Are we putting our total trust in the Lord and His money that He gave us? No. If He can take care of the small sparrow then surely to goodness, the Lord will provide for us as well. In 1905, Mrs. Civilla Martin and her husband were visiting a couple in New York. Mrs. Doolittle was bedridden for twenty years and her husband was confined to a wheel chair. Their hopefulness and faith intrigued Dr. Martin. He asked Mrs. Doolittle, "What is your secret?" She replied: His eye is on the sparrow and He watches over me. The next day Mrs. Martin submitted a poem to Charles Gabriel. He supplied the music and that's how the old church hymn came about entitled, "His eye is on the sparrow." God never sleeps. He watches over us 24 hours a day, 7 days a week every day of the year. All you have to do is trust him and thank Him!

Prayer for today: *Heavenly Father, Thank you so much for watching over me each and every day. In Jesus' name, Amen.*

What's in a Name?

Over our summer vacation, we were in Florida and while traveling on our way back home we almost had an accident along with several other cars. We were the ones who caused it. We had a roof rack on our car with a kayak tied down to it and in an instant the wind carried it off and behind us cars swerved off the road to try and avoid it. No one was hurt, but it was a very scary dilemma. One lady hit our boat and had a flat tire. We got off the next exit and immediately turned around to go help and see what we could do. A department of transportation worker stopped to help us. Guess what his name was? His name was Jeremiah. I knew after he told me his name we were all going to be just fine. We ended up giving our boat to Jeremiah and money to the lady with the flat tire. We were bummed about the boat with no way to get it back home but thankful no one was injured. I talked with Jeremiah briefly and asked him had he ever read the bible verse Jeremiah 29:11. He said no but said that he would look it up on his cell phone after we left. In the bible, God tells us that

Security

Jeremiah was called to be a prophet. He was set apart. In Jeremiah 1:5, it says the following: Before I formed you in the womb, I knew you, before you were born, I set you apart; I appointed you a prophet to the nations. Jeremiah was strong, courageous, faithful, and obedient to the Lord. I wonder when his mother had him did she know of the book in the bible about Jeremiah. When I told my mom of the accident, she asked me if we were all ok. I said, "yes God sent Jeremiah to help us." My first son's middle name is David. It is a family name passed down from his father's middle name. I feel sure it was chosen from the bible in reference to King David. David had a heart for God. He was a king who led God's people by God's principles, and God blessed him greatly. I can only hope one day that my Preston David will have a heart for God in the same manner. My other son is named, "Adam". "His name came straight from the bible as you must know in Genesis. His name is special because it was the first name chosen by God. Also, in the book of 1 Corinthians 15:45 it says: So it is written: "The first man Adam became a living being"; the last Adam, a life-giving spirit. The second Adam is referring to Jesus. I pray our little Adam will grow up to be the Christian man, father, and husband that God has called him to be. The next time you are introduced to someone and they tell you their name, dig a little deeper. There just might be some meaning on that name to give you some insight worth investigating.

Prayer for today: *Heavenly Father, I pray that you*

will help me to grow my children that you have given me up to be Godly examples for your glory! In Jesus' name, Amen.

Security

Genuine

Roots

While driving to town today I noticed a tree that was on the edge of a bank. You could see its roots below the ground level for at least fifteen to twenty feet. I thought man those roots really run deep. Isn't that how it is with the roots of bitterness? Have you ever been bitter toward someone and you just can't seem to shake it? With friends, having bitterness toward someone it's easy to just stop being friends and find new ones. However, with family you can't do that as easily. Have you ever held a grudge toward someone? Can't seem to forgive them? In Hebrews 12:15 it says: See to it that no one falls short of the grace of God and that no bitter root grows up to cause trouble and defile many. If you just stopped talking to that person, it would not be enough because the bitterness is still there. Just like the root. If you simply cut it in half it is still there and can grow back. You have to dig the entire root up to prevent it from growing back. Unless you completely forgive, another person that has wronged you the bitterness will never go away. God says we must forgive. In Matthew 6:15 it says: But if you do not forgive others their sins, your Father will not forgive your sins. It's easy to make mistakes. In Romans 3:23 it says: for all have sinned and fall short of the glory of God. Even though we fall short, God forgives us through his grace. Ephesians

1:7 says: In him, we have redemption through his blood, the forgiveness of sins, in accordance with the riches of God's grace. Acts 13:38 says the following: Therefore, my friends, I want you to know that through Jesus the forgiveness of sins is proclaimed to you. If we are to be like Christ, don't you think it's time to get out your gardening tools and dig those roots up? Pray for God to forgive you for being bitter. Pray for God to soften your heart towards that person. Pray for God to help you get past the past and look toward the future. If it's someone who can't forgive you and has pretty much written you out of their life then all you can do is ask for forgiveness, pray, and leave it God's hands. My knees have been dirty from digging up roots, but now I can wear my Sunday best with a smile. Praise the Lord!

Prayer for today: *Heavenly Father, if there is any bitterness in my heart today, cleanse me of right this second so that I can have a pure heart and walk in your pathway. In Jesus' name, Amen.*

Silver Refinement

I don't have very much jewelry in my jewelry box that's worth a whole lot. I have mostly costume jewelry and what is really expensive I wear. Nowadays, most women don't wear the popular gold jewelry, but wear silver instead. I have both, and am fond of both. In doing research on the history of silver I have found it dates back several centuries. In biblical times, silver was very common. People not only used it for jewelry, but other things as well such as plates, bowls, candlesticks, cups and even coins, which they referred to as shekels. The word silver is mentioned in the King James Version of the Bible three hundred and sixty times. It was first mentioned in Genesis 13:2 And Abram was very rich in cattle, in silver, and in gold. It was found in the earth according to Job 28:1 it says: There is a mine for silver and a place where gold is refined. It was found in an impure state and had to be refined. In Proverbs 25:4 it says: Take away the dross from the silver, and there shall come forth a vessel for the finer. In Zechariah 13:9 it says: And I will bring the third part through the fire, and will refine them as silver is refined, and will try them as gold is tried: they shall call on my name, and I will hear them: I will say, It is my people: and they shall say, The Lord is my God. In Numbers 31:22-23 it says: Only the gold, and the silver, the brass, the iron, the tin, and the lead, Everything that may abide the fire, ye shall make it go through the fire, and it shall be clean: nevertheless it shall be purified with the water of separation: and all that abideth not the fire ye shall make go through the water. In Malachi 3:3 it says: He will sit as a refiner and purifier of silver; he will purify the Levites and refine them like gold and silver. Then the Lord will have men who will bring offerings in righteousness,. When a refiner is purifying silver he sits in front of the fire holding the silver over the fire. The silver can't be over just any part of the fire it must be in the hottest part of the, fire the center of the flame. This is where the impurities get burned away. The refiner has to sit there watching the silver the entire time that the silver is in the flame. You ask: why he has to sit there? The reason is that if the silver is left a moment too long the silver will be destroyed. Not only does the refiner have to sit there the entire time he must watch the silver the entire time. If he doesn't watch it the entire time it will be very easy to leave it in too long. He will not take his eye off the silver or the fire. But how do you know when the silver has been fully refined? It is ready to come out when you can see your image in it reflects the image of the refiner. Wow! God is our refiner. We are His piece of silver. He allows us to go in the firey trials of this life and reach a certain temperature but will not take his eye off of us! He wants to put us through the fire so that he can see his reflection in us. We are to be made in his image. How long have you been in the fire? Are you ready to come out and cool off? Or did you come out for a little while, only to be put right back in? Until you completely surrender yourself, he is going to keep you in the middle of the fire. He's looking for his reflection in you. Are you ready to shine for Jesus? I am.

Prayer for today: *Heavenly Father, thank you for putting me through the fire to make me who I am today. I am stronger. I am thankful that you are my refiner and will never take your eyes off of me. Continue to take out the impurities in me, so that I will only shine for you. In Jesus' name, Amen.*

What defines you?

Lately I have been looking at different people and wondering to myself, "What is it that defines them?" When I'm driving and get behind a car that has a bumper sticker on it, then it usually is a dead giveaway. Weather its sports, religion, or they are a proud parent of an honor roll student, you can pretty much read their identity and what they want others to know about them. Sometimes people wear what they are focused on such as their favorite home team, polo shirts, or by the way they dress. I recently sat down and talked to a good friend of mine, Liz, who also just happens to be my editor. When I see her, usually she has on her workout clothes, tennis clothes, or she's dressed to the hilt looking very radiant. We talked about, "What defines people". Looking on the outside you see that she enjoys tennis, must love to work out and has herself very much altogether when she's out in public. What I didn't know about her was the reason why she does what she does. She plainly told me, "I try my best to take care of my body, because in scripture we are told it is a temple in which Jesus resides." Now if I didn't know that, I may have thought something entirely different about her. So with all that said, let's take a quick glance at what God's word says about our identity. God created us in His image which was a good thing!(Genesis 1:26-27) Since we are a reflection of God and His image, we should carry around with us His character, and self worth and know that He values us greatly. Our identity in Christ should be what defines us if we are a Believer and follower of Christ. John 1:12 says "Some people did accept him. They believed in his name. He gave them the right to become children of God." Colossians 2:13 says " At one time you were dead in your sins. Your sinful nature was not circumcised. But God gave you new life together with Christ. He forgave us all of our sins."

If you truly come to repentance of your sins whole-heartedly then you will be one with the spirit of the Lord. His spirit will dwell in you. You will be so in tune with Him that you hear Him speak to you and direct your paths. He will become your identity - when others see you, they will see Christ. 1 Corinthians 15:22 says "Because of Adam, all people die. So because of Christ, all will be made alive." As Christians we are a new person. We no longer walk in the fleshly worldly ways or have the same desires. God plants a new seed in our very core of our being, and once he does it takes a lifetime to mature. Warren Weirsbe once wrote, " Knowing that you belong to the one Lord, that you have received the one faith delivered to you and that you have experienced the one baptism of the Holy Spirit, then Christian unity will be a rich blessing in your life. When you worship and serve the one God who is your Father, the God who is sovereignly at work in all things, then the minor differences among Christians will not prevent you from enjoying and strengthening the unity of God's people." If you are a Christian, then Jesus Christ defines you and that is your identity as a reflection for all to see.

Genuine

Prayer for today: *Our Father in Heaven, forgive us of our sins. Come into our hearts and minds and give us a double portion of your Holy Spirit. Help us to recognize that we can't change our past in the flesh, but we can change our present and our future through Jesus Christ and the Holy Spirit within us. For I pray this in Jesus' name, Amen.*

Home Sweet Home

Sometimes I find myself praying for God to watch over our house and put a hedge of protection around it continuously. I know the enemy can prowl around like a roaring lion just waiting to destroy our home. If our house is one that God is the head of then I'm sure Satan would like to see it crumble. He doesn't care to go after people who do not practice Christianity in their homes.

He already has them where he wants them, so why bother? He wants to destroy everything we've worked so hard to build. We are his challenge. In the book of Proverbs 24:3 it says the following: By wisdom a house is built, and through understanding it is established. How do you get wisdom to run your household? You get wisdom by staying in God's word daily and He will tell you how to run it. If the enemy comes knocking on your door, you better make sure you know how to guard yourselves. He can come in through television, music, and the computer. He can come through people that you are in contact with. All he needs is someone to be a tool for him and get in your mind.

If he gets the right emotions of anger, dissension, depression, bitterness, and un-forgiveness surrounding you or a family member then he succeeds. All it takes is one family member in the house to have any one of those characteristics and your home has disruption lurking in the air. In Joshua 24:15 it says the following: But as for me and my household, we will serve the LORD. He knew that his whole household needed to worship God and Him alone. He knew that if he kept his covenant with the Lord that God would bless his house. He had a pleasing aroma to God. He warned the people that God was a jealous God and if they didn't renew their covenant with Him, then God would destroy everything they worked so hard for. His home was, "Home Sweet Home". Can you say that about yours?

Prayer for today: *Dear God, make our home pleasing to your sight and be a sweet aroma to you. Put a hedge of protection so thick full of thorns surrounding our home that the enemy cannot get through. Fill our walls and each and every room with your holy spirit. In Jesus' name, Amen.*

House Divided

Have you ever driven by someone's house during football season and seen a flag out front that shows two different teams on it? That means their house is divided. One person is pulling for one team and the other person for somebody totally opposite!

83

Sometimes when you are married to someone who is not on the same spiritual level as you are the house may seem divided. Or, maybe one person is sold out and surrendered to the Lord and the other person doesn't have a clue what that means yet, then it means the house is divided. It is definitely a struggle between both people involved. In biblical terms, it means you are unequally yoked if one person is a Christian and the other is not. If that's the case then one of you will have a hard row to hoe so to speak. I have known women who divorce because they can't take their spouse not being the Godly man he was called to be. I have known women who give up and get out of their Christian walk completely because they are tired. I have known women who pray and stay until God intervenes. I have known women who go to a different church than their spouse because they couldn't agree. Praise they stay married! In the bible it says in the book of 2 Corinthians 6:14 it says: Do not be yoked together with unbelievers. For what do righteousness and wickedness have in common? Or what fellowship can light have with darkness? John MacArthur quoted the following: "Believers and unbelievers inhabit two opposing worlds. Christians are in Christ's kingdom, which is characterized by righteousness, light, and eternal life. Unbelievers are in Satan's kingdom, characterized by lawlessness, darkness, and spiritual death. The saved and the unsaved have different affections, beliefs, principles, motives, goals, attitudes, and hopes. In short, they view life from opposing perspectives. My grandmother told me years ago, stay in church and He will follow. She was married fifty-two years. She was a woman of wisdom! In Peter 3:1 it says: Wives, in the same way be submissive to your husbands so that, if any of them do not believe the word, they may be won over without words by the behavior of their wives.. I can tell you from my experience that having a house divided is more than just the football teams. It's spiritual warfare and a constant battle. For the believer, stay in the word daily, play Christian music, cut off the television, and pray without ceasing. Always be prepared for battle as it says in Ephesians. One day just when you least expect it your spouse will surprise you and show up in church, broken before the Lord with their bible in hand. All the years of praying will have paid off, the struggling forgotten and soon you will realize you are no longer divided but on the same team!

Prayer for today: *Heavenly Father, I pray that you will always be the Head of our Household so it will not crumble. I pray that you will keep your holy spirit in and through every room of our home. I pray that you would protect our home with a crown of thorns so thick that the enemy can't get through. In Jesus' name, Amen.*

Wise

Happy Hour

I know a man who is well up in his years who looks to his local bar for comfort. He is lonely and I can't imagine why he continues year after year to drink alcohol to try and take away his pain. What's so happy about it? Is it the fact that they give you free food when you order a drink? Is it the fact that the people around you are all drinking with you, so that means they are in agreement with you? I know everyone has their own opinion and not everyone is under the same conviction. If you drink, let me just say I am not judging you. This is a decision that is something you have to make on your own.

Let's take a look at what the bible says about drinking alcohol. I Corinthians 10:31 states "Whether therefore ye eat, or drink, or whatsoever ye do, do all to the glory of God." To me, it would be pretty hard to witness to someone about Christ with a drink in my hand, thinking clearly and glorifying God at the same time. It's no secret that wine in the New Testament very often meant simply grape juice. In the Old Testament the word for wine and grape juice was the same. Contrary to what many believe, Jesus didn't turn water into alcoholic wine (John 2:3-10) because He would be contradicting a multitude of Scriptures in the Old and New Testament regarding this subject. In verse 10 of John 2 chapter 3, they had already "well drunk" up to this point. Jesus had to make a decision; either contribute to the drunkenness that would surely follow with that much wine or just say no. After all, the Bible does say that no drunkard shall inherit the kingdom of God (I Corinthians 6:10). That would be a contradiction in why Jesus came to the earth in the first place...to save all of mankind.

Another violation of scripture Jesus would have been guilty of breaking is found in Habakkuk 2:15a which states "Woe unto him that giveth his neighbour drink, that puttest thy bottle to him, and makest him drunken also". Jesus creating and serving 100-150 gallons of alcoholic wine clearly goes against this Scripture. My conclusion is that it was fermented water (grape juice) in order that they would be able to drink it. In I Timothy 5:23 it states "Drink no longer water, but use a little wine for thy stomach's sake and thine often infirmities." Paul was not talking about drinking socially or in moderation. He was using it as a medicine because the water was not clean. Most people today don't understand that wine (grape juice) in Biblical times was greatly watered down and served to preserve the purity of water. "They that tarry long at the wine; they that go to seek mixed wine. Look not thou upon the wine when it is red, when it giveth his colour in the cup, when it moveth itself aright (Proverbs 23:30-31)." This passage says don't even look at wine once it has turned to strong drink. This is God's message to believers even before they attempt to take a drink. You may be surprised to find that the word "beer" is used in the Bible. In the New International Version of the Bible the Hebrew word "shakar" is translated as "beer". In the King James versions of the Bible the Hebrew word "shakar" is translated as "strong or intoxicating drink." They made these drinks from dates or other fruits (grapes excepted) or barley millet, etc. Proverbs 20:1 says "Wine is a mocker and beer a brawler; whoever is led astray by them is not wise." This tells me that wine, beer nor any alcoholic beverage is "ok" in God's eyes. Romans 14:21 says " It is good neither to eat flesh, nor to drink wine, nor any thing whereby thy brother stumbleth, or is offended, or is made weak." With all of this said, is "Happy Hour" really worth risking becoming an alcoholic or contributing to someone else who might become one? After all it always starts with just one drink, right?

Prayer for today: *Heavenly Father, I pray that I will not give in to worldly ways, but set an example to others that glorifies You and You alone. In Jesus' name, Amen.*

Good Eye

Earlier this year when my son was playing baseball and he would go up to bat you could hear his teammates in the background say, "Good eye". They were referring to how he judged the ball and how he knew when not to swing. Then my little one sometimes will notice when the dog has something in her mouth and we don't see it. Good eye. Alternatively, think of when you're traveling

and you miss a car that is driving recklessly and you are able to avoid a serious accident. Good eye. What about when you've lost something important and your spouse comes along and say "Is this you were looking for?" Good eye. Well, in all of those instances to have a good eye is a requirement.

When thinking of a good eye spiritually you have to have the Holy Spirit as your guide and follow and trust in God's word. You can pretty much know when the enemy is attacking you because once you become a Christian the bible says you are set apart. The enemy comes like a roaring lion waiting to devour you. (1 Peter 5:8) Be alert and of sober mind. Your enemy the devil prowls around like a roaring lion looking for someone to devour. Don't let it be you!

When in conversation with someone who points out your every mistake and is quick to judge you and bring you down keep your mouth shut and remove yourself from the situation. Not only can that come from a person who is your friend, often it's from your own flesh and blood. Key word is flesh! When we are not living in the ways of Christ Jesus to the best of our ability our flesh and sinful nature gets the best of us. It can get us from anything such as jealously to gossip. You must keep your eyes focused on the Lord and know when the enemy is attacking. (Proverbs 15; 3) The eyes of the LORD are everywhere, keeping watch on the wicked and the good. If the eye is the window to your soul then work on making it a "good eye ".

Prayer for today: *Father God please help me to always see through the eyes of Jesus. In His name I pray, Amen.*

Divine Appointments

Isn't it great when God orchestrates an appointment for you? One time I met a good friend who was in my Sunday school class. She came to visit one day. She didn't have anywhere to sit. I had a seat next to mine and she sat down. She then didn't have a pen. I offered her mine with a smile. The next week her mom asked her if she was coming back. She told her she would if the girl that offered her the pen would be there. I was there and we became good friends and had a lot in common. Another time I was at a bible study picnic in a park. The study was about to begin and there was a lady who just happened to show up with two of her children to eat their lunch. I went over, introduced myself, and invited her and her children to join us. She did and that day both of her children got saved and came to know Christ. God knows our agenda each and every day before we plan it out. I am so grateful for that. Early this morning I was reading in the book of Ruth. God had a divine appointment for Ruth to meet Boaz. She had no idea that he would be the one to help her or would be her future helpmate and husband. However, God knew. Boaz was her kinsman redeemer. He met her in the fields as she was gathering the sheaves. He rescued her. In Ruth 3:9 it says: "Who are you?" he asked. "I am your servant Ruth," she said. "Spread the corner of your garment over me, since you are a kinsman-redeemer." A kinsman redeemer was one who volunteered to take responsibility for the extended family. Boaz was her nearest relative to take care of her. Jesus is our kinsman redeemer. He came to earth as a man to save us. He redeemed us from our sin. Isn't that awesome! Last year I signed up for a bible study called, "Women at War" at our church. I had no idea it was a divine appointment. The woman who taught the class in such a way moved me closer to God more than I could ever have imagined. After her class, I started serving more in ministry. I met some great Godly friends. She helped me break the chains of bondage I had struggled with emotionally for over 25 years! God had her on my agenda and I had no idea. In Habakkuk 2:3, it says the following: For the revelation waits an appointed time; it speaks of the end and will not prove false. Though it linger, wait for it; it will certainly come and will not delay.

Today I am looking for a divine appointment to help, comfort, pray, and love on someone in need. I wonder who's on your calendar.

Prayer for today: *Heavenly Father, I pray that you will always help me to see a "Divine Appointment" scheduled by you on my daily calendar. In Jesus' name, Amen.*

The Number Forty

Today is my husband's birthday. He is now forty years old. When I think of that number I reflect on my life. I think that it wasn't until I reached forty that I truly started living for God. The number forty is so significant that it's mentioned several times throughout the bible. Moses spent forty years in Midian for killing an Egyptian

Wise

soldier. The Israelites wandered around in the wilderness for forty years for being disobedient to God. Noah had to wait forty days after it had already rained forty days and forty nights before opening the window. Jesus was tempted forty days. Jonah gave Nineveh a forty day warning of judgment. The Roman soldiers gave forty lashes as their method of punishment. Elijah after eating one meal was strengthened to go forty days to Mount Horeb where he heard the voice of God. Jesus after he was crucified was seen on earth for forty days. Moses was on the mountain of God for forty days (twice) and when he came down his face shone with light for forty days. For forty days Goliath antagonized the Israelite army before David killed him. Isaac was forty when he married Rebekah. Solomon reigned for forty years. Esau was forty years old when he married Judith. I'm sure there are more times the number forty is used. It was a turning point in my life. I woke up and realized my purpose and that I was to bring God Glory. That's why he made me. That's why he made you. I stopped going through the motion and started living for God. Are you tired from going around the mountain in the wilderness? Are you tired of being hungry and never being filled? Let the number forty be a turning point in your life. Wake up and realize where you've been and turn toward God. He's given you a purpose in your life. He's given you eternal life through Jesus. Look at the gift he gave you. Won't you come to him and share that gift with others? Isaiah 43:7 says the following: everyone who is called by my name, whom I created for my glory, whom I formed and made." Today I celebrate with my husband his birthday. I pray that it is a turning point in his life to live for King Jesus and that he will have a burning desire to glorify God in all that he does.

Prayer for today: *Heavenly Father, I pray that you would help my husband stay on your path, seek you daily, and be the husband and father you have called him to be. In Jesus' name, Amen.*

Three Days

Recently our son Adam (who is seven) took swimming lessons. The instructor guaranteed in three days to have him swimming. By the third day he knew how to jump off diving board, swim under water, open his eyes and swim using his arms and legs to get to the side of the pool. Amazing, absolutely amazing! Or is it? One of my friends gave me the best advice one time. When I can't make a decision she told me to wait and pray for at least three days. Very sound advice. Also, this past week I decided to do a fast for at least three days. I did it and was so grateful. I meditated on God's word for once. I lost three pounds and had so much energy. It was very gratifying, to say the least.

You know there is a lot of scripture about "three days" in God's word. For instance, God told Joshua to go around the camp and get his people ready because in "three days" he would cross the Jordan river. In the book of Exodus Moses stretched out his hand and darkness covered Egypt for "three days". Esther 4:16 says "Go, gather together all the Jews who are in Susa, and fast for me. Do not eat or drink for three days, night or day." Matthew 12:40 says "For as Jonah was three days and three nights in the belly of a huge fish, so the Son of Man will be three days and three nights in the heart of the earth. Man will be three days and three nights in the heart of the earth." Acts 17:2 says "As was his custom, Paul went into the synagogue, and on three Sabbath days he reasoned with them from the Scriptures." Mark 14:58 says "We heard him say, 'I will destroy this temple made with human hands and in three days will build another, not made with hands.'" John 2:19 Jesus answered them, "Destroy this temple, and I will raise it again in three days." Luke 24:7 says "The Son of Man must be delivered over to the hands of sinners, be crucified and on the third day be raised again."

A lot can be accomplished in three days, but nothing compares to the resurrection of Jesus Christ on the third day! Three days was a significant amount of time in the eyes of God. God set the pace to perfection, because in three days, "It was finished!"

Prayer for today: *Heavenly Father thank you for sending Your son to die and rise again on the third day in order to save those You love so much. Please forgive me of my sins. Continue to open my ears to hear, my eyes to see and keep them focused only on You and what Your will is for my life. In Jesus' name, Amen.*

Great Strength

Yesterday I noticed my teenager lifting weights outside. He is sixteen years old and is trying to change the way he looks by defining his muscles. Of course, spring break is coming up and I'm sure the beach has something to do with it. What he doesn't understand, like most teens at his age, is how great strength comes from within. What does God's word say about strength? In Exodus 15:2 Moses and the Israelites sang a song to God, including this verse: "The LORD is my strength and my defense, he has become my salvation." In the book of Judges, Samson prayed for great strength to push down the pillars and kill the Philistines. God answered his prayer. David said in Samuel 22:33 "It is God who arms me with strength. Surely God is my salvation; I will trust and not be afraid." Isaiah 12:2 says "Surely God is my salvation; I will trust and not be afraid. The LORD, the LORD himself, is my strength and my defense; he has become my salvation." In Ecclesiastes 9:16 it says "So I said, 'Wisdom is better than strength.' But the poor man's wisdom is despised, and his words are no longer heeded." Daniel 10:18 says "Again the one who looked like a man touched me and gave me strength." In 1 Peter 4:11 it says "If anyone speaks, they should do so as one who speaks the very words of God. If anyone serves, they should do so with the strength God provides, so that in all things God may be praised through Jesus Christ. To him be the glory and the power forever and ever. Amen."

Wise

It is obvious our true strength comes from God! In Warren Wiersbe's book *Be Strong* ,he writes of Joshua and his strength. "God isn't looking for volunteers, because every Christian is a soldier in the army of the Lord. Some are 'good soldiers of Jesus Christ' while others are AWOL or casualties on the battlefield of life. Joshua was one of God's early soldiers on the winning side. Thrust into leadership when Moses died, Joshua took to heart God's instructions about the keys to victory. Putting fear aside and realizing the Lord was his true source of strength, Joshua became God's instrument for bringing the Israelites safely into the Promised Land."

I'm praying my son will realize one day that it is not what is on the outside. It is what is on the inside. His great strength will not come from pumping iron, but from the Lord!

Prayer for today: *Dear Heavenly Father, may I always rely on You for my strength in everything I do. In Jesus' name, Amen.*

Fair Trade

Last night I had the pleasure of playing referee between my two boys. The oldest one was being the clever con artist to the youngest one. Preston told Adam, "If you sell me your red hat, I will give you $ 20,000 dollars in monopoly money." Preston then said, "Let's shake on it." He extended his hand, and that's when I walked in the room. Wait! Luckily, I saved Adam from losing his favorite hat just in the nick of time! It reminded me of being tempted. God says in 1 Corinthians 10:13 "No temptation has seized you, except what is common to man." God is faithful - He will not let you be tempted beyond what you can bear. But when you are tempted, He will also provide a way out so you can stand up under it. If you are walking with God you can see the way out, just as Abraham did right before he was about to kill his son Isaac. God provided the ram, and Abraham took notice and sacrificed it instead. However if you are not walking with God, you just might sell your birthright for a bowl of stew as with Esau and Jacob. That one deal between brothers not only cost Esau losing his inheritance, but several generations suffered as well. What my teenage son does not know is that God hates shady deals. In Deuteronomy 25:16 it says "For the LORD your God detests anyone who does these things, anyone who deals dishonestly."

To make sure any business dealing is a "fair trade" we must first evaluate everything involved. What will the lasting effects be? Will it glorify God? Will anyone get hurt in the process? Will it hurt me in any way? Will it take away from God or my family? A hat to you may not seem that big of a deal, but to my little one its one he treasures. You know why? Because when he wears it, it reminds him that his daddy bought it for him. It reminds him that his daddy has one just like it. Preston did not know those things. Thomas Brooks once wrote "A well-grounded assurance is always attended with

three fair handmaids: love, humility and holy joy."
Next time someone offers you a fair trade, make
sure it's done with good intentions and pray about it.
While you are waiting, God just may show you if
it's really best or not.

Prayer for today: *Heavenly Father, please teach me
to wait and pray before my "yes is a yes." Give me
wisdom and discernment in knowing what is best for
me. Thank you Father for watching over me and
helping me to make wise choices. In Jesus' name,
Amen.*

Protecting our Own

This month there was a helicopter shot down
by the Taliban in Wardak Province, Afghanistan.
Thirty men were killed. Twenty-two were Navy
Seals. My heart goes out to the families. In the book
of Ecclesiastes, it states there's a time for peace and
there's a time for war. In Joshua 11:18 it says: that
he waged war against all these kings for a long
time. Our nation says that we are one nation under
God. Are we really? I think we need a revival!
When it comes to protecting our own not only does
it apply to the soldiers protecting our country, it
applies to our individual families and friends. In
Psalm 5:11 it says: But let all who take refuge in
you be glad; let them ever sing for joy. Spread your
protection over them that those who love your name
may rejoice in you. God will protect us if we are
obedient to him. He will watch over us until it is our

time to be called home to Heaven. When we turn our security alarm on at night, we are protecting our family. We are putting up a shield around our home. We are protecting our family from the enemy. In Ephesians 6:16 it says: In addition to all this, take up the shield of faith, with which you can extinguish all the flaming arrows of the evil one. Are you protecting your soul? Are you guarding your heart? Proverbs 4:23 says the following: Above all else, guard your heart, for everything, you do flows from it. So many preachers agree that we are in the end times right now and Jesus could come back at any time. I think it's time for us to band together and reach out to all who need protecting and are in need. We need to bring back prayer in our schools. We need to fill up the church and have a revival. We need to ask God for forgiveness. How can we protect our country if we just stay in our own little world? Do we really need that star bucks every day? I have to admit I do love coffee, but I can think of a lot of sandwiches that one cup would cost and feed the homeless with it. Webster's Dictionary defines protection as supporting one who is weaker. Who needs protection? Everyone from the enemy. If you allow Satan to attack you, he will snuff out your flame. Always be on guard, take up your shield of faith, and trust in the Lord. When someone is weak, they need help. Won't you help protect them and lift them up? All it takes is the hands and feet of Jesus and you will find your light shining brightly.

Prayer for today: *Heavenly Father, I pray that will*

give me wisdom and discernment in order to help protect my family, friends, and strangers from the enemy. In Jesus' name, Amen.

Cell Phone Ceasing

We are in a world of so much technology right now that we have forgotten how to have an old fashioned conversation eye to eye, face to face. My son texts messages so much that I'm afraid one day when he goes on a job interview he will want to text the employer instead of meeting them in person! How many times have we gone down the road and just feel like now would be a good time to talk to someone. We are driving. We pick up our cell phones and call somebody just to have someone to talk to. If they don't answer then we call someone else. We are suppose to be driving for goodness sake! I am guilty just the same. I do not choose my time wisely and I need direction and constant self control in that department. Instead of picking up the phone and dialing someone to talk to, why not dial God? He's always listening. He never sleeps. He will lend an ear. If it's really quiet and you are listening without the background noise, you just might hear him speak back to you. When Samuel was sleeping God woke him up three times before he realized God was talking to him. In 1Samuel 3:10 the bible says the following: The LORD came and stood there, calling as at the other times, "Samuel! Samuel!" Then Samuel said, "Speak, for your servant is listening." It took God three times to

101

get Samuel's attention. How many times does it take God to get ours? Are we listening attentively for him to call us? Or are we so wrapped up in talking with our friends, listening to music, and the news that we are deaf? The next time you are anxious to talk to someone with excitement, try calling God instead. I'm sure he's listening and will be delighted you called. In John 9:31 it says the following in the bible: We know that God does not listen to sinners. He listens to the godly person who does his will. In 1John 5:14 it says the following in the bible: This is the confidence we have in approaching God: that if we ask anything according to his will, he hears us. God doesn't have a number that you have to put on your contact list. You don't have to look down at your phone and thumb through your contacts to find him. All you have to do is say," Lord", and he's there.

Prayer for today: *Heavenly Father, I pray that you would help me to always call on you first before seeking out others and listen for your response. In Jesus' name, Amen.*

Gift of Teaching

Yesterday, I had to sign up my teenager for a college prep test and call a tutor for him. It seems like he has grown up so fast! I can't believe he is getting ready for college. Where in the world did the time go? My youngest son is struggling with reading right now so today I am going to check on a tutor for him as well. Do you ever need extra help for yourself or your children when life gets difficult? What do you do when you start to pull your hair out after going over the same spelling words with your child for almost three hours and he still doesn't get them? Sometimes we all need extra help from someone else every now and then. In the bible in Ephesians 4:2, it says this: Be completely humble and gentle; be patient, bearing with one another in love. My gift is not patience so if I ever know that I am being patient I know it is coming from God! To be a teacher or tutor requires a great deal of patience. In Luke 6:40 it says the following: The student is not above the teacher, but everyone who is fully trained will be like their teacher. While Jesus walked from town to town most of the people called him, "teacher". He was training them to be a better person.

Even, his disciples referred to him as a teacher. He kept their attention by using everyday objects and illustrations. He used methods to draw them near to him and keep their attention. He was and still is one of the greatest teachers ever known. Crowds would surround him and be so engrossed in his teaching that they would forget to eat. He would then perform a miracle and sustain their hunger. I do not have the capability to keep either of my children's attention focused on me for very long. Just when I was about to throw in the towel and get a tutor for my little Adam as well, I had my oldest son sit down and teach him his spelling words last night. Amazingly, Adam listened to him. Preston used a different method than I did the day before and within fifteen minutes Adam knew four spelling words! Preston has the patience of Job! I don't and when I tried to teach Adam I just got frustrated. Jesus had patience. It was his character. He knew what would draw a crowd, how to get their attention, and how to make them believe with astonishing faith! "Come unto me, all ye that labor and are heavy laden, and I will give you rest. Take my yoke upon you, and learn of me; for I am meek and lowly in heart; and ye shall find rest unto your souls. For my yoke is easy, and my burden is light." —Matthew 11:28-30. Charles Spurgeon once wrote in reference to that verse the following: Now I think the Savior says to us, "I am bearing one end of the yoke on my shoulder; come, my disciple, place your neck under the other side of it, and then learn of me. Keep step with me, be as I am, do as I do. I am meek and lowly in heart; your heart must be like mine, and then we will work together in blessed fellowship, and you will find that working with me is a happy thing; for my yoke is easy to me, and will be to you. Come, then, true yoke-fellow, come and be yoked with me, take my yoke upon you, and learn of me." If that is the meaning of the text, and perhaps it is, it invites us to a fellowship most near and honorable. If it be not the meaning of the text, it is at any rate a position to be sought after, to be laborers together with Christ, bearing the same yoke. Such is our lot. Jesus invited, taught light heartedly, and offered his mercy. He set the example of how we are to teach with discipline, love, patience, and understanding.

Prayer for today: *Heavenly Father, I pray that you will give me patience in teaching my children. Forgive me Father for not exemplifying your character. May you continue to pour out your Holy Spirit in me daily so that I can shine for you. In Jesus' name, Amen.*

Wise

Fishermen

Today while watching my husband fish on the pier I noticed he was getting frustrated while wondering why he wasn't catching anything. On the other side of the pier, some retired gentlemen were catching fish left and right. My husband wanted me to ask them what their secret was so I did. I watched them first and then asked. They gave us advice on what bait, what fishing weights, and what type of pole to use. Now my husband will know next time and hopefully will have better luck in the future. He needed advice from someone more seasoned. Isn't that the way it was with Jesus. In Mark 1:17 it says: Come, follow me," Jesus said", and I will send you out to fish for people". They had to follow him because he was the only way they would ever learn what it meant to be humble. In Luke 5:4-7 it says: When he had finished speaking, he said to Simon, "Put out into deep water, and let down the nets for a catch". Simon answered, "Master, we've worked hard all night and haven't caught anything. But because you say so, I will let down the nets." When they had done so, they caught such a large number of fish that their nets began to break. Therefore, they signaled their partners in the other boat to come and help them, and they came and filled both boats so full that they began to sink. In John 21: 4-6 it says the following: Early in the morning, Jesus stood on the shore, but the disciples did not realize that it was Jesus. He called out to them, "Friends haven't you any fish? " No", they answered. He said, "Throw your net on the right side of the boat and you will find some." When they did, they were unable to haul the net in because of the large number of fish. Jesus knew when and where for them to let down their nets. When they listened to him, they caught so many fish they were astonished. He said he would make us fishers of men if we would follow him. How many are you reeling in for Jesus? Are you following him enough to be able to be an example to others? Have you even tried to cast your net out? Charles Spurgeon once wrote the following: We must live his life and be ready to die his death, if need be. O brothers, sisters, if we do this and follow Jesus, putting our feet into the footprints of his pierced feet, he will make us fishers of men. We are called to follow Him. His holy spirit will guide our net as to where it should be cast out. All we have to do is be willing.

Prayer for today: *Heavenly Father, help me to be a fisherman and bring many souls to come to know you. In Jesus' name, Amen.*

Wise

Zealous

Christianity

I just had a conversation with someone I dearly love about what is the definition of a Christian and what other religions believe. I have to go the biblical route. I believe a Christian is a follower of the Lord Jesus Christ. A Christian is associated with a true visible evidence of God's grace.

(His undeserved kindness) A Christian is also associated with being a disciple. (A true follower of Christ) In Acts 11: 22, 23, 26 it states that when Barnabas arrived at Antioch he saw the grace of God. He was glad. He explained to them a need for a wholehearted commitment for the Lord. ...The disciples were called," Christians" at Antioch. Barnabas saw Gods grace through a visible change in the people there. The word Christian is associated with a change in lifestyle (demonstrated by ones actions). If one claims to be a Christian and keeps going around the mountain for 40 years making the same mistakes will they ever see the Promised Land? In Acts 26:20-23, 27, 28 Paul says we must change the way we think and act and our deeds must show the fruits of a changed heart. He then says that we must accept the message of the prophets. In 1 Peter 1:6-9, 4:12-19 the word Christian is associated with a willingness to share in Christ's sufferings. If we didn't suffer, how would we ever experience Joy? Knowing that King Agrippa didn't intend to call Paul a Christian as a complement meant that if you were a Christian you were willing to suffer. A person had to be seriously willing to suffer if they wanted to be a disciple of Jesus Christ. Are you willing? You can choose the modern way of thinking and claim to be a Christian regardless of what you believe or do; or you can choose the New Testament concept. You can choose to be a follower of Jesus Christ, have a changed way of thinking and living, have a willingness to accept what the bible says, and have a willingness to suffer for Christ. If you are willing to change your life for Christ and go through some suffering for Him he will bless you beyond measure. I'm not perfect; I'm a sinner and make mistakes. However, I have been forgiven by Gods grace through his son Jesus. Knowing that where I once was in my life was a deep dark pit and the only way out was the touch of Jesus hand makes me want to share the gospel with others so they can know they don't have to stay in the pit. You have a Savior too. His name is Jesus.

Prayer for today: *Father in Heaven thank you for saving me through your son, Jesus. May I continue to share the Good News of your love? In Jesus' name, Amen.*

People in Our Pathway

In Savannah, GA, I met a woman by the name of "Lou". She was born in Lebanon and came to the states thirty-five years ago. She resides in Wisconsin. She was visiting for a few days alone just to see the city. She came by rail on Amtrak. I admired her for getting out of her home and seeing God's creations. She seemed to be well into her sixties and said that she had two grandchildren. She said she still wanted to travel while she was still able. I got to witness to her about my faith in Jesus Christ. I love how God puts people in your pathway. Just maybe she was supposed to be in mine as much as I was in hers. Remember when Jesus decided to take an alternate route to Samaria in John 4? He met the woman at the well. What a life changing conversation!

Today in St. Augustine, I spent some time with my grandfather. Before I left, he asked me to pray with him. He prayed with my grandmother every night before she died earlier this year. It was something he cherished. It was something he looked forward to. I'm grateful I got to share in a moment that was sacred to him tonight. Although he is still hurting, I think God arranged for me to be here to help comfort him today. Who knows what God has in store for tomorrow? Who will cross our pathway? Whether it is a stranger who needs Jesus or a friend, or a family member I believe God sets the divine appointments on our agenda each and every day. It is up to us to look, listen and seek out the perfect opportunity to be an ambassador of Christ.

2 Corinthians 5:20 says the following: We are therefore Christ's ambassadors, as though God were making his appeal through us. Since not everyone around us holds up a sign that tells us how we can pray, comfort, or help them it should be our job to find out. We all at one time or another may not have gone through the same trial in this life but I guarantee you we have shared the same emotion. The next time you have been placed in someone's pathway, it just may be God's almighty hand that placed you there.

Prayer for today: *Heavenly Father, I pray that I will always represent you no matter where I travel so that I can shine for Jesus. In Jesus' name, Amen.*

On a Mission

Today I felt like a missionary set out to share the gospel. I had my new release of my book in hand and I was walking in and out of shops to try and introduce my book. God gave me the words and the courage to deliver a message of redemption. I sold four books. I talked with an owner who allowed me to put some of my books in her shop on the counter. I also gave the community center my name to call me for a book signing and speaking engagement. Although I am tired, it's a good tired. I had to think and wonder did Paul feel the same way by chance. One Sunday in church our Pastor said that Paul was one of the greatest missionaries of all time. Every town he went to he shared his testimony of how Jesus turned his life around. Charles Spurgeon once wrote about Paul. He said the following: Oh! if you could have seen Paul preach, you would not have gone away as you do from some of us, with half a conviction, that we do not mean what we say. His eyes preached a sermon without his lips, and his lips preached it, not in a cold and frigid manner, but every word fell with an overwhelming power upon the hearts of his hearers. He preached with power, because he was in downright earnest. You had a conviction, when you saw him, that he was a man who felt he had a work to do and must do it, and could not contain himself unless he did do it. He was the kind of preacher whom you would expect to see walk down the pulpit stairs straight into his coffin, and then stand before his God, ready for his last account. What Spurgeon was saying is this: you have to be on fire for the Lord to be a missionary! You have to have zeal for the Lord and want to share the gospel of Jesus with anyone God places in your pathway! Romans 12:11 says this: Never be lacking in zeal, but keep your spiritual fervor, serving the Lord. I have a friend named, Tony who has zeal for the Lord. He has been on several mission trips sharing the gospel. When he's stuck here in his hometown he doesn't meet a stranger. He will talk to anyone about Jesus he comes in contact with. While he's waiting at a restaurant, he talks to the waiter. While at a store, he talks to the cashier. While waiting on the tow truck, he talks to the mechanic. He doesn't meet a stranger and neither did Paul! 1Corinthians 9:19 says: Though I am free and belong to no one, I have made myself a slave to everyone, to win as many as possible. That's my goal. I want to reach many with my testimony in order to give people hope through Jesus!

Prayer for today: *Heavenly Father, send me on a mission for your glory in order to help save souls that are lost. Give me your holy spirit, your words, and zeal for you like none other! In Jesus' name, Amen.*

Loving Loud

This weekend our church truly "loved" on our community in a huge way! Everyone used their talents to help donate their money and their time. They gave out free health exams, haircuts, car repairs, painting, landscaping, blankets, clothes, food, and so much more that the list goes on and on. They call it "LoveLoud". For one weekend out of the year they really pull together to get things done. Everyone has an opportunity to serve, no matter what the age. They help out with orphanages, shelters, schools, single moms, widows, soldiers, nursing homes, etc—...How is this possible? God.

He is the Shepherd. You see he has a plan to get things accomplished for his glory. He uses people to make sure his sheep are taken care of one way or another. In the Bible in John 10:14, it says the following: "I am the good shepherd; I know my sheep and my sheep know me— He has also set the example for us to follow in his footsteps. It says in 1 Peter 5:2 it states: Be shepherds of God's flock that is under your care, watching over them—not because you must, but because you are willing, as God wants you to be; not pursuing dishonest gain, but eager to serve; God wants us to serve, but to have a cheerful heart doing so. When you are filled with the Holy Spirit, it's automatic. He is our pilot and guides us to do the right thing, with the right attitude at heart. Romans 15:15 it says this: May the God who gives endurance and encouragement give you the same attitude of mind toward each other that Christ Jesus had,...In the Bible it also states in Ephesians 6:7 the following: Serve wholeheartedly, as if you were serving the Lord, not people,... We are called to serve as if serving our Lord. In the Bible in Colossians 3:24 it says: since you know that you will receive an inheritance from the Lord as a reward. You are serving the Lord Christ. Someone once told me, "Bloom where God plants you." I am so glad the Lord our Shepherd has placed me in such a wonderful church and community where I can serve alongside others with a grateful heart. I was once a weed, but now I'm blooming into an awesome flower right where I'm planted and "loving" every minute of it!

Prayer for today: *Heavenly Father, I pray that you will help me to see that I can love others all year long and bring them help, hope, and healing. In Jesus' name, Amen.*

Without Excuse

I know of two people who have lived past ninety years old. Both of them do not know Jesus as their personal Lord and Savior. Can you imagine going through this life with all of the sickness and pain that we have to endure and never feeling the hope, and love of Jesus Christ? Some people might think well, I'm a good person so I'll make it into heaven. Others may think, well I'm going to earn my way in by serving others. The Bible says in Romans 1:20 the following: For since the creation of the world God's invisible qualities—his eternal power and divine nature—have been clearly seen, being understood from what has been made, so that people are without excuse. Some people may say, "Oh, I believe in God and that's enough." Actually, no it isn't enough. In the book of John 14:16 it says: Jesus answered, "I am the way and the truth and the life. No one comes to the Father except through me. Serving others is good, but having faith goes with it. Someone once told me an illustration about being in a boat and trying to get to the other side of the lake. One oar represented "serving". The other oar represented, "faith". If you just used the serving oar only, the boat would spin in a circle. If you use both serving and faith together you will get too the other side of the lake. In Galatians 2:16 it says: know that a person is not justified by the works of the law, but by faith in Jesus Christ. So we, too, have put our faith in Christ Jesus that we may be justified by faith in Christ and not by the works of the law, because by the works of the law no one will be justified. Because I have faith in God through Jesus Christ, He leads me to do His will. Today along with friends and family, I got to pray with people I didn't even know. It was a rundown housing project.

The Lord was with us and we provided his word along with sandwiches for them. It felt good to serve. I could see the hurt, the desperation, the sickness, and the uncertainty in their eyes. I got to hug them and let them know we cared as we prayed for them. The Holy Spirit was present and it was a good feeling. I want to go back. I want to do more. I have the desire to please and serve our Lord. I am now without excuse. He has equipped me with his Holy Spirit and my salvation is solid and secure. Knowing we ought to do and not doing it is sin. Forgive me Lord of my shortcomings. Here I am, Send me.

Prayer for today: *Heavenly Father, I pray today that you will always help me to see others with your heart and through your eyes. In Jesus' name, Amen.*

Telling About Jesus

Tomorrow for the first time in a long time, I will stand before several women and give my testimony. I have been practicing, writing, and rewriting. I've come to one conclusion in my prayer closet this morning. God will give me the words to speak when it's time to speak. He will speak through me what I need to say in order to glorify him. I think about people in the bible, who when it came time for them to speak, what did they do. In the book of Exodus it says this: But Moses said to the LORD, "Since I speak with faltering lips, why would Pharaoh listen to me?" Moses had doubts,

117

but God had a back up. He sent his brother Aaron to speak on his behalf. Then I think of Jonah. When God told him to go to Nineveh, he ran. He got thrown overboard, swallowed up by a big fish, and then God got his attention. It was only then that he obeyed after God spoke to him a second time. In the book of Jeremiah 26 it says: "This is what the LORD says: Stand in the courtyard of the LORD's house and speak to all the people of the towns of Judah who come to worship in the house of the LORD. Tell them everything I command you; do not omit a word. Perhaps they will listen and each will turn from their evil ways. It seems to me that to tell the people about Jesus is Gods very plan in order to save them. Last but not least, let's take a look at John. In Acts 13 it says: Before the coming of Jesus, John preached repentance and baptism to all the people of Israel. As John was completing his work, he said: 'Who do you suppose I am? I am not the one you are looking for. But there is one coming after me whose sandals I am not worthy to untie.' John was telling about Jesus before he even arrived to the people to prepare them for the one they have longed for. Prophets before him did the same thing. In the book of Acts 13:46 it says this: Then Paul and Barnabas answered them boldly: "We had to speak the word of God to you first. Since you reject it and do not consider yourselves worthy of eternal life, we now turn to the Gentiles. For this is what the Lord has commanded us. "'I have made you a light for the Gentiles, that you may bring salvation to the ends of the earth.' When the Gentiles heard this, they were glad and honored the word of the

Lord; and all who were appointed for eternal life believed. 1Corinthians 1:17 says: 'For Christ sent me not to baptize, but to preach the gospel.' Oswald Chambers stated the following about that verse: The one passion of Paul's life was to proclaim the Gospel of God. He welcomed heart-breaks, disillusionments, tribulation, for one reason only, because these things kept him in unmoved devotion to the Gospel of God. That's how I feel. I am ready today to share my deepest, darkest sins and let anyone know who will listen how God redeemed me from my past through Jesus Christ. I may be nervous, but it's not enough for Satan to stop me!

Prayer for today: *Heavenly Father I pray that you would give me a triple portion of your holy spirit in order to have courage to stand for you in front of anyone you put in my pathway. Open the doors wide open for me to walk through and share the love of Jesus. In His name, Amen.*

Zealous

119

Grief

Carrying the Weight

Sometimes we have heavy burdens that seem very hard to carry. I have talked with a lot of people over the past several months. I ask them how can I pray for them and just listen to what their response is and then turn it over to the Lord. I have met people who have cancer, lost loved ones, are dealing with custody issues over their children, have a child in prison, have children who are very sick, have parents who are in their later years and are having to take care of them, have rebellious teens, job loss, depression, marriage problems, fear, anxiety and the list goes on. All of these things mentioned to me are very heavy burdens. Honestly, I don't know how anyone can get through this life without God. 1 Peter 5:7 says "Cast all your anxiety on him because he cares for you." God is waiting for us to seek Him to turn over our concerns and worries to Him. He knows the weight we carry, He just wants you to trust in Him enough to know that He is in control. James 4:10 says "Humble yourselves before the Lord and He will lift you up." Psalms 145:14 says "The Lord upholds all those who fall and lifts up all who are bowed down." Matthew 11:28 says "Come to me, all you who are weary and burdened, and I will give you rest. Take my yoke upon you and learn from me for I am gentle and humble in heart, and you will find rest for your souls. For my yoke is easy and my burden is light."

The invitation is open to all who are willing to trust in Jesus that He can help share the heavy yoke with us so that we don't have to pull the burden alone. Oswald Chambers once wrote "If we did not know some Christians well, we might think from just observing them that they have no burdens at all to bear. But we must lift the veil from our eyes. The fact that the peace, light, and joy of God is in them is proof that a burden is there as well. The burden that God places on us squeezes the grapes in our lives and produces the wine, but most of us see only the wine and not the burden. No power on earth or in hell can conquer the Spirit of God living within the human spirit; it creates an inner invincibility." John 14:27 says "Do not let your hearts be troubled and do not be afraid." No matter what burden we are carrying, God cared enough to send his son, Jesus, to carry the weight at the cross so we are not alone.

Won't you trust in him today, and make your load a little lighter?

Prayer for today: *Heavenly Father, the burdens are many but I am trusting in You to carry every single one. May You make my load a little lighter by walking alongside me and when I am too weak to walk, carry me. In Jesus' name, Amen.*

Unclouded Day

Yesterday our family attended the funeral of a loved one. He left behind two boys and will be greatly missed. Don was a former Marine, a hard worker and always wore a smile. He was often the first one to offer help to anyone that needed. He was in a band called, "Twang" and played the guitar beautifully. At the graveside, his band played his favorites and one of them was called, "Unclouded Day". Don chose to take his life this past week and end it tragically. On the outside everything must have seemed fine, but on the inside he was dying. As the band started playing, just in perfect harmony the clouds poured out the raindrops. It was a sad day not only filled with rain but teardrops in mourning his loss for everyone in attendance. I'm not sure why God allowed this to happen, but I can tell you that with every bad thing that happens, God will turn it around for something good and His glory every single time. God's word says He will never leave us nor forsake us. He will not let us be plucked out of His hands. Although Don chose to end his life, perhaps it was God's will to allow it to happen in order to save those that are lost around him. This made me reflect on that particular song tremendously. Why was it a favorite of his, I wondered. The song was written by Josiah Alwood, who was a circuit rider preacher. He was away from his family often and rode horseback from town to town having revivals. On a moonlit night he wrote the lyrics. Later he turned them over to an editor of a music journal, "The Echo" who published it for him somewhere around 1880. The hymn portrays the beauty of Heaven. The song later appeared in a book entitled Living Gems. Some of the lyrics are as follows: Stanza 1 says that heaven is a home far beyond the skies

"O they tell me of a home far beyond the skies, O they tell me of a home far away; O they tell me of a home where no storm clouds rise, O they tell me of an unclouded day." In the scriptures, heaven is pictured as being far beyond the skies, in heaven. It is also pictured as a home, a dwelling place that Jesus is preparing for His people. While there will be no storm clouds, it is the place from which Jesus will descend in the clouds: Rev. 1.7 "O they tell of a home where my friends have gone, O they tell me of that land far away, Where the tree of life in eternal bloom, Sheds its fragrance through the unclouded day." Heaven is land that now seems far away, but it is a country that God has promised His people: Heb. 11.13-16 O they tell me of the King in His beauty there, And they tell me that mine eyes shall behold Where He sits on the throne that is whiter than snow, In the city that is made of gold." The King is obviously Jesus Christ, who promises that we shall sit with Him on His throne: Rev. 3.21 "O they tell me that He smiles on His children there, And His smile drives their sorrows away; And they tell me that no tears ever come again, In that lovely land of unclouded day." His smile will drive all their sorrows away so that there will be no tears in heaven: Rev. 21.4 The concept of the "cloudy day" represents all the things that cause crying and pain, so without such things heaven will be a place of "unclouded day" with God Himself as the light: Rev. 21.22-25 We will hold onto the hope we have in Heaven where there will be no more sorrow or pain on that Unclouded Day.

Prayer for today: *Heavenly Father, I am holding on to the hope You have promised us. That hope gives me the courage to press on for the prize that awaits us. I pray that as we run the race You have laid out for us that we will draw close to You, gain strength from Your word, so that we can lead others to You so you can save them through your son, King Jesus. Thank you for loving us enough to save us through Your gift of grace in your son. Bring us comfort and peace in knowing we will meet those who have gone on before in Heaven. In Jesus' name, Amen.*

Questionable Healing

This morning I woke as many times to spend my quiet time with God and I had to wonder as I'm sure many do, Why are some people healed by God and others with the same faith not? Why are some people that are unbelievers healed and others that are not? While searching through scripture it's plain to see that in the Bible there are verses that revolve around Faith. However, Paul was a great man of faith, he had asked for healing, and God chose not to heal him.

(2 Corinthians 12:7-9) In the book of Hebrews 11:32-39 All of the prophets and great men of the Bible were all commended for their faith. It was the will of God for each of them to live out each circumstance in their life to reflect on that person and those around them at that very given point and time. God has chosen to be glorified by the healings of some and to be glorified by taking others through sickness and hurt. Look at Job. God is still concerned even though He doesn't intervene immediately in every situation. I am not sure why God keeps me in stitches so to speak wondering why He spared my son and in the future, if He will one day choose to take him. I do know that my children are a gift to me. They were lent to me from God to take care of to the best of my ability even if it is for just a short while. He can choose to take them from me at any given moment. They are ultimately "His" children. We as believers are to trust God in whatever circumstance we are given. We are to pray to be delivered, and healed. We are to do all that we can to try and solve the situation. We are to realize that God has an overall plan that we as humans may not understand in our lifetime. Jeremiah 29:11 For I know the plans I have for you, declares the Lord, plans to prosper you, and not to

harm you, plans to give you hope and a future. My son told me one day, "Mom don't worry because I'm not". (He was saved and baptized when he was six years old.) He said," If I die I know I am going to be with Jesus and I will get a new body." One day he was in the kitchen and the radio was playing the song "I'll fly away"...It brought tears to my eyes when I looked and noticed he was singing the song. I have learned to take things one day at a time. Sometimes the doctors have it down to a science and other times God steps in and "Wow's them without an explanation. Thank you Lord for keeping them on their toes, for giving me strength beyond measure, for loving me, and saving such a wretch like me. Weather God heals us on earth, or heals us when we get to Heaven He is God almighty, God of wonders, and He never stops!

Prayer for today: *Heavenly Father, thank you for your healing hands. May you continue to watch over me and my family. Heal those that need healing and comfort those that need comfort. In Jesus' name, Amen.*

Running from God

Yesterday my church bible study looked at Jonah. That story made me think of a few people that I know. No matter how much you love them or pray for them, they still keep running in the opposite direction from God. Why is that? Do they just not want to give up their worldly pleasures? Is drinking to get drunk, idolizing men, or money, or cars, looking like a million bucks with hair, clothing, makeup, or that new home that has to look like Better Homes and Gardens really worth the exchange of their salvation? No! So what happened to Jonah when he acknowledged God and was given instructions by Him, yet he didn't do it? Jonah ran from God and set sail away from Nineveh hoping that God would just forget about the whole ordeal and send someone else to tell the people there of their evil ways. God called Jonah.

Have you ever been called to do something and not follow through? There are consequences for that, right? Jonah 1:17 says "Now the LORD provided a huge fish to swallow Jonah, and Jonah was in the belly of the fish three days and three nights." Even though Jonah ran, God still provided. Jonah then prayed to God and He had compassion for Jonah. He made the huge fish spit Jonah out on dry land right near Nineveh! Jonah then did what the Lord asked him to do. Jonah 3:3 says "Jonah obeyed the word of the LORD and went to Nineveh. Now Nineveh was a very large city; it took three days to go through it. Jonah then warned the people that Nineveh would be overthrown in forty days if they did not turn to the Lord." God taught Jonah a lesson of not obeying Him. There is nowhere that you can hide from God, hide your sin and not be found from God Almighty. Isn't the three days that Jonah was in the fish the perfect picture of the death, burial and resurrection of Jesus? Matthew 12:40 says "For as Jonah was three days and three nights in the belly of a huge fish, so the Son of Man will be three days and three nights in the heart of the earth." Jonah ran from God and went to sleep. God however, never sleeps. Charles Spurgeon wrote " If nothing else had awoke Jonah, the prayers of the mariners ought to have awakened him; and the earnestness of your mother and father, the pleading of your sister, the cries of new converts, the earnest anxieties of enquirers, ought to have — and if you were not so deeply sunken in slumber, would have some influence over you to arouse you."

Jesus is coming. Are you running in His direction or running away from Him? You cannot seek the love of God while running from God. He's awake 24/7 with arms wide open, a listening ear and a heart waiting for you. Won't you say, "I'm tired of running God", and let Him direct your path?

Prayer for today: *Heavenly Father, I pray that if I ever start to run in the opposite direction from Your will for my life that You will wake me up and point me in the right direction. I pray today for many who are running away from You, that they will turn toward Jesus before it's too late. In Jesus' name, Amen.*

Holding on to the Power of God

My oldest son has to go in the hospital this week for a liver biopsy and further testing to see why his liver is showing signs of rejection. This is not the first time. Actually, this is probably the eighth time he has had a biopsy. We have been to our local children's hospital numerous times over the past twelve years. He had a liver transplant at age four. He is now almost seventeen. This time in particular, his bile duct is narrowing and may require a stent to open it up. I asked him the other day, "Are you worried or scared this time?" He replied, "It's all I've ever known." That one reply made me think of the many people who were sick who had an encounter with Jesus during his time on earth. Imagine living your whole life with a disease such as leprosy, seizures, blindness, and one encounter with Jesus will cure you for life! Matthew 9:35 says "Jesus went through all the towns and villages, teaching in their synagogues, proclaiming the good news of the kingdom and healing every disease and sickness."

Once when my son was much younger and we were in the hospital, things looked very dim. His P.E. teacher called and asked me to put my hands on his stomach while she prayed through the phone. The next morning the doctor told me he couldn't explain it, all of his labs came back normal and he was sending us home. James 5:15-16 says "And the prayer offered in faith will make the sick person well; the Lord will raise them up. If they have sinned, they will be forgiven. Therefore confess your sins to each other and pray for each other so that you may be healed." The prayer of a righteous person is powerful and effective. Now, knowing that, I'm not sure why he is not completely healed. I do know that it may not be God's will. I also know He will use something bad for His Glory. If he is not completely healed here on earth, he will be in heaven. Revelation 21:4 says "He will wipe every tear from their eyes. There will be no more death or mourning or crying or pain, for the old order of things has passed away." Romans 8:28 states "And we know that in all things God works for the good of those who love him, who have been called according to his purpose." Warren Weirsbe wrote in reference to the leper in Psalms 88 "The foundations of his life seem to be slipping away, and the possibility of death looms before him. In his desolation, what does he do? He holds on to God's power, loving-kindness and faithfulness." That is exactly what we shall do as well. We will hold on to the fact that whatever happens to our son, it is for God's Glory and is His plan for his life. Trusting God brings peace and power to a tired weary soul.

Prayer for today: *Heavenly Father, I am placing my faith and trust in You today. I pray for healing where there needs to be healing, for forgiveness where there needs to be forgiveness, and I am thanking you in advance for what You are doing in and through my life. I lift up Preston to you today, as well as many who are suffering from sickness. I pray that You will heal them Father by the touch of Your hand. In Jesus' name, Amen.*

Joy/Love

Learning to Praise Him

Recently I went to a concert at our church. As I was singing to the music, I also could hear a child's voice close by singing as well. I looked to my right and a little girl named, "Lexie", with straight black hair, wearing a blue dress, and a white sweater was singing to the top of her lungs. (She was only seven years old, I later found out.) She was as cute as could be singing, standing and waving her hand as high as she possibly could. It made me smile just watching how much she enjoyed praising God. She didn't care who saw her with her hands lifted high or whose view she may have been blocking. She simply loved God and was there to worship. Aren't we supposed to have that same mentality? Mark 10:15 says "Truly I tell you, anyone who will not receive the kingdom of God like a little child will never enter it." After all, God sent Jesus to save us and pay our sin debt. He endured tremendous pain and died on the cross for us. By the grace of God, He gave us eternal life through Jesus. Isn't He worthy to be praised? Psalm 145:3 says "Great is the Lord and most worthy of praise; his greatness no one can fathom."

What does the Bible says about lifting your hands? Psalms 135:2 says "Lift up your hands in the sanctuary and praise the Lord." Psalm 28:2 says "Hear my cry for mercy as I call to you for help, as I lift up my hands toward your Most Holy

Place." 1 Timothy 2:8 says "Therefore I want the men everywhere to pray, lifting up holy hands without anger or disputing." Charles Spurgeon once wrote "Uplifted hands have ever been a form of devout posture, and are intended to signify a reaching upward towards God, a readiness, an eagerness to receive the blessing sought after. We stretch out empty hands, for we are beggars; we lift them up, for we seek heavenly supplies; we lift them towards the mercy seat of Jesus, for there our expectation dwells." I just love that!

Our expectation dwells in the hope of Heaven that only comes through Jesus Christ our Lord and Savior. The next time you're in church or at an event where you are freely able to worship God, try closing your eyes and think about thanking Him for saving your soul from spending eternity in Hell. If you do, I can almost guarantee that before long you will be praising Him just like a little child without a care on the world with hands lifted high.

Prayer for today: *Heavenly Father I thank you for loving me, for forgiving me of my sins, and I pray that You will continue to teach me how to worship and praise You even if it's through the eyes of a child. In Jesus' Name, Amen.*

Welcome to the Family

I have met two different families this past week who have adopted children. The first family was a single mom named Tarsa who had two boys. One boy was hers and the other she had adopted from her girlfriend before she died. She was fortunate to get all legal paper work signed in order to adopt the boy before his biological mother passed away. She made reference to how proud she was now that both boys were in college. Her face lit up as she spoke about "her boys" and you could tell how much she loved them. The other family was a lady named Carol who is a nurse. She and her husband adopted twin girls from China when they were just ten months old. Both girls are in high school now and love gymnastics. When talking of their children, both moms referenced the children as their own as if they had carried them nine months themselves. It made me think of how we are adopted in the family of God once we become believers of Christ. God calls us His children, His sons, His daughters, His very own heirs through the Holy Spirit once we receive Christ as our Savior. Galatians 4:4-7 says "But when the set time had fully come, God sent his Son, born of a woman, born under the law, to redeem those under the law, that we might receive adoption to sonship. Because you are his sons, God sent the Spirit of his Son into our hearts, the Spirit who calls out, "Abba, Father." So you are no longer a slave, but God's child; and since you are his child, God has made you also an heir." Romans 8:14-17 says "For those who are led by the Spirit of God are the children of God. The Spirit you received does not make you slaves, so that you live in fear again; rather, the Spirit you received brought about your adoption to sonship. And by him we cry, "Abba, Father." The Spirit himself testifies with

Joy/Love

our spirit that we are God's children. Now if we are children, then we are heirs —heirs of God and co-heirs with Christ, if indeed we share in his sufferings in order that we may also share in his glory."

Thinking of adoption also reminded me of when I went to Secret Church to hear David Platt. He talked about when he adopted his daughter, Mara Ruth. He coincided it with Jesus being our redeemer. Pastor David Platt, author of "Radical", said it best when he wrote the following "We who were children of wrath become children of God! But it's not just our legal status that has changed. When God transforms our status, He also changes our family. He calls us a new name (John 1:12-13), He gives us a new spirit (Romans 8:16), and He grants us complete access into His presence (Hebrews 4:14-16)." He continues, "Whereas we used to be afraid of God our Judge, we are now friends of God our Father! As His children, God promises us a full inheritance in His family. We are fellow heirs with Christ Himself, and His is an inheritance that will never spoil or fade. When God adopts, He doesn't adopt temporarily; He adopts eternally. His adoption of us is literally forever!"

I can truly say my redeemer lives and I am so thankful I have been adopted into the family of God and I hope that you are too.

Prayer for today: *Heavenly Father, thank you for reminding me this week that we are Yours through Christ and are heirs to the throne! In Jesus' name, Amen.*

Light in the Darkness

We are on vacation and as I look off my balcony, the lighthouse shines brightly in the dark of the night. It has been shining since 1872 and guiding ships safely to their destination. I love lighthouses. They remind me that God is mine. He is my light in the darkness and guides me where I need to go. In the bible in 2 Samuel 22:29 says the following: O Lord, you are my lamp. The Lord lights up my darkness. So many people who do not have a relationship with Jesus walk around in the darkness. In John 12:35 it says the following: Jesus replied, "My light will shine for you just a little longer. Walk in the light while you can, so the darkness will not overtake you. Those who walk in the darkness cannot see where they are going. I can't imagine living on this earth and never knowing the love of Jesus. So many people who go through trials in their life never see the joy on the other side after the trial is over without him. In John 8:12 it says the following: Jesus spoke to the people once more and said, "I am the light of the world. If you follow me, you won't have to walk in darkness, because you will have the light that leads to life." Years ago one time I called my grandmother. She found out that I loved lighthouses and she made a copy of a hymn and sent it to me. It was entitled, "The Lighthouse" by Ronnie Hinson. After receiving it in the mail, I called her to thank her. We then started singing through the phone and it was a sweet memory. I will never forget her voice as she sang. She was full of joy even though she had

Joy/Love

been through so many trials in her life. She was a breast cancer survivor. She had lost a child and gone through divorce. Where did her joy come from? Jesus. She looked to him as her light to get her through the darkness. I am so thankful for the legacy she left behind. In John 1:5, it says the following: The light shines in the darkness, and the darkness can never extinguish it. No matter what she went through, her light never went out. I can only hope that my children and grandchildren will say the same about me. If it wasn't for the lighthouse, where would this ship be?

Prayer for today: *Heavenly Father, I pray that I will always let my light shine before men! I pray that you will never let the enemy snuff it out and that you will fill me daily with a triple portion of your holy spirit. In Jesus' name, Amen.*

Harvest Time

I can remember years ago spending my summers at my grandmother's house and getting up early to go out in the garden. We would pick cucumbers, squash, beans, okra, corn, and pull up potatoes out of the ground. Sometimes I got to ride on the back of the tractor that my grandfather would use to till up the soil. Sometimes I got to learn how to shell peas, string beans, and shuck silver queen corn. I learned a lot from my grandparents about that garden. The best benefit of all was sitting around the table and enjoying the meal together. In the book of Psalms 107:37-38 it says the following: They sowed fields and planted vineyards that yielded a fruitful harvest; he blessed them and their numbers increased and did not let their herds diminish. In Matthew 9:37 it says: Then he said to his disciples, "The harvest is plentiful but the workers are few. In Romans 1:13 it says : I do not want you to be unaware, brothers and sisters, that I planned many times to come to you (but have been prevented from doing so until now) in order that I might have a harvest among you, just as I have had among the other Gentiles. The Lord desires us to be the farmers for him. We are to go into the fields and bring in the harvest. So many people are in desperation who doesn't know that they have a Savior in Jesus who can save them and give them hope. In John 4:35 it says: Don't you have a saying, 'It's still four months until harvest'? I tell you, open your eyes, and look at the fields! They are ripe for harvest. It's time to get up early, to go out in the garden, and bring in the bounty for our Lord. What a day it will be when we can all feast with our Lord and worship at his table. Matthew 22:9 says: So go to the street corners and invite to the banquet anyone you find.' Won't you bring others into the family of God? All you have to do is invite them.

Prayer for today: *Heavenly Father, I thank you for reminding me of the harvest and the example my grandparents set. May I sow many seeds and bring others to know you! In Jesus' name, Amen.*

Apple of My Eye

When my oldest son was little it was easy to
see that, he was the apple of my eye. I adored his
hugs and kisses. As he gets older, they fade away
and instead of walking beside me and holding my
hand, he keeps his distance. Now I have a six year
old and he has somewhat taken his older brother's

place. He hugs me every morning and kisses me goodnight before bedtime. I have truly been blessed with two amazing children. Although my oldest one is now seventeen, driving, dating, and sleeping late we still find time to talk. He asks my opinion on things and we watch movies together. He still tells me he loves me and that's enough for me. My youngest one keeps me in stitches with practical jokes. He is an early riser just like me. He is so sweet and has such a tender heart. They are both different and years apart yet they never argue. They find time to play games together and that makes me very happy. They are both the apple of my eye. They are God's gift to me and I treasure them dearly. Do you ever wonder since we are God's children if we are the apple of His eye? In Proverbs 7:2, it says the following: Keep my commands and you will live; guard my teachings as the apple of your eye. In Deuteronomy 32:10, it says: In a desert land, he found him, in a barren and howling waste. He shielded him and cared for him; he guarded him as the apple of his eye. In Psalms 17:8 David is praying to the Lord and says the following: Keep me as the apple of your eye; hide me in the shadow of your wings. I honestly think that the Lord delights in us just as much as we do our own children. When we obey him, trust in him, and love others it must please him. God protects his children just as we protect ours. In Zechariah 2:8, it says the following: For thus said the Lord of hosts, after his glory sent me to the nations who plundered you, for he who touches you touches the apple of his eye. Do me a favor, won't you? The next time you slice an apple cut it horizontally and when you open it up you will find a perfect star. To me that's just a little hint that there's always more than meets the eye.

Prayer for today: *Heavenly Father, thank you for the gifts you've given me in my children. I am grateful to you for giving me two sons that I delight in daily. In Jesus' name, Amen.*

Sweet Aroma

I met a new friend by volunteering in her neighborhood a few months ago. Every time, I saw her she just seemed like she was trying to get out of her current situation. My heart went out to her because I've been there. She was depressed and embarrassed for the way things were. She recently lost her job and told me she just wanted her house cleaned. So today a friend of mine helped me get her apartment clean and we helped her haul off a lot of clutter. We gave her a study bible she had asked me for, and when we left she was smiling. Her apartment was clean and had that lemon fresh clean smell. I told her if Jesus were to knock on her door, he would smell a sweet aroma!

In the book of Numbers 28:33 it says "Give this command to the Israelites and say to them: 'Make sure that you present to me at the appointed time my food offerings, as an aroma pleasing to me.'" In the Old Testament, the sacrifice was the pleasing aroma to God. In 2 Corinthians 2:15-16 it says "For we are to God the pleasing aroma of Christ among those who are being saved and those who are perishing. To the one we are an aroma that brings death; to the other, an aroma that brings life." And who is equal to such a task? In the New Testament, we as Christians are the pleasing aroma. Oswald Chambers wrote "We are encompassed with the sweet aroma of Jesus, and wherever we go we are a wonderful refreshment to God." Adrian Rogers once wrote "When we are praising God in the midst of trials, singing songs of glory in the midst of persecution, claiming His victory when a problem arises, then we are emitting a sweet aroma that is unmistakable to the nostrils of God. This is the sweet smell of victory!"

If you put the love of Christ on daily, you will bring joy to everyone you come in contact with and make this world a lot brighter!

Prayer for today: *Heavenly Father, I just love You and want to share Your love and light with others. I pray that I will be a pleasing aroma to you wherever I go. In Jesus' name, Amen.*

Jealous for Me

This week I heard a song entitled, "How He Loves", by David Crowder Band. In the lyrics, the song says he is jealous for me. Have you ever thought about how God is jealous for you? It made me think that He wants my undivided attention. He longs to spend time with me. He loves me that much. In the Bible in Exodus 34:14 it says the following, "Do not worship any other god, for the LORD, whose name is Jealous, is a jealous God. When he says do not worship any other God, he's talking about anything you put before Him. That includes family, money, job, television, computer, and friends just to name a few. He longs for us to spend time with him and develop a relationship with him. Webster's dictionary for the word idol is the following: An image or representation of anything. In 1John 5:21 it says the following: Dear children, keep yourselves from idols. The Lord is very jealous for your love. Charles Spurgeon once wrote the following: He cannot endure that you should think you are your own, or that you belong to this world. He loved you with such a love that he could not stop in heaven without you; he would sooner die than that you should perish; he stripped himself to nakedness that he might clothe you with beauty; he bowed his face to shame and spitting that he might lift you up to honor and glory, and he cannot endure that you should love the world, and the things of the world. Our Father in Heaven deserves our love, our trust, and is worthy to be praised! He laid down his life for you and me. He gave the ultimate sacrifice. Does it bother you when your loved one does not give you your undivided attention? I can't tell you how many times it irritates me when I try to talk to my teenager. I call his name several times. He does not hear me. He is texting his friends, watching television, or playing video games. The last thing he wants to do is listen to me. I am jealous for his love. I can only imagine how much more God is jealous for me! This month of November, I am thankful for God that he was so jealous for me that he sent his son to die for me. He wanted to clothe me in beauty and take away my sin and death that I deserve. In the book of Songs of Solomon 8:6 it says the following: Place me like a seal over your heart, like a seal on your arm; for love is as strong as death, its jealousy unyielding as the grave. It burns like blazing fire, like a mighty flame. Green is my favorite color. Now when I see it, it reminds me of His jealous love burning for me.

Prayer for today: Heavenly Father, I pray that you will always remind me that you long to spend time with me and are jealous when I put others and objects before you. Forgive me O Lord and help me to stay focused on you and you alone. In Jesus' name, Amen.

Grateful Heart

How do you know if someone is doing something for you with a grateful heart willingly or out of obligation? I have been very blessed by a lot of older and wiser women in my life. As I sit back and watch them, no doubt they have shown me hints of their grateful heart and how to use it. Both of my grandmothers had the gift of mercy, which was passed down in our family. My mother had it as well. For years, my maternal grandmother would give cards for every resident on every Holiday of the year to her local nursing home. She would give on top of her required tithe, money to others in need, and to St. Jude's Hospital every year. She passed down the card ministry to my mother, who then passed it down to me. My paternal grandmother would give her tithe, bake, and cook for others as well as sew. I have known people who give, but seem to expect something in return. They do it out of obligation without a grateful or cheerful heart. In the Bible it says in 2 Corinthians 9:7 Each of you should give what you have decided in your heart to give, not reluctantly or under compulsion, for God loves a cheerful giver. I have even known someone a time or two who has given me something and then asked for it back. What's the point? Honestly, if someone does something for you, don't you want to know that they went out of their way, not expecting anything in return and wants to bless you? In Deuteronomy 15:10 it says the following: Give generously to them and do so without a grudging heart; then because of this the LORD your God will bless you in all your work and in everything you put your hand to. In Exodus 25:2

144

it says the following: "Tell the Israelites to bring me an offering. You are to receive the offering for me from everyone whose heart prompts them to give. Key word is prompts. Does your heart prompt you to give? Or, do you have to analyze the situation and see if you will benefit from it first? Luke 10:27 says the following: He answered, "'Love the Lord your God with all your heart and with all your soul and with all your strength and with all your mind' ; and, 'Love your neighbor as yourself.' " If you loved your neighbor as much as you do yourself, then there would be no room for pride, selfishness, or thinking the world owes you something. You would not think twice about helping someone in need or taking too much time to see if it's the right thing to do. Once Jesus deposits his Holy Spirit in you, you start to look at everything with a grateful heart and are eager to walk in his ways.

Prayer for today: *Heavenly Father, teach me your ways, never let me hold a grudge, forgive me if I have, and help me to see everyone through your eyes with a grateful heart. In Jesus' name, Amen.*

Gifts from God

My little boy received his very first real Bible from our Pastor at our church recently. He was so excited and ready to highlight everything with his brand new highlighter. He wanted his picture taken with his bible, and when it was time for bed, he wanted me to read out of it instead of his picture

bible. I can't tell you how much that made my heart happy! Don't you think it's the same with God and his children? He desperately wants us to come to him eagerly, willingly, and with a desire to want to know him. In the bible it says in the book of

Isaiah 54:3 it says: All your children will be taught by the LORD, and great will be their peace. In Proverbs 22:6, it says the following: Start children off on the way they should go, and even when they are old, they will not turn from it. I am grateful to share Gods word with my children. I know they are going to have pressures in life that pull them away from God, but deep in their heart Jesus resides and they will come back to Him if they stray away. I think of the Sheppard when one of his sheep gets out of line and he takes the rod and pulls him back. It's hard to let go of our children but knowing they are Gods children and are our gift just for a little while makes a huge difference. Luke

18:16 says this: But Jesus called the children to him and said, "Let the little children come to me, and do not hinder them, for the kingdom of God belongs to such as these." James Dobson once wrote:

Children are not casual guests in our home. They have been loaned to us temporarily for the purpose of loving them and instilling a foundation of values on which their future lives will be built. I am grateful for my boys. Although they are ten years apart, they love each other, and both are the fingerprints of God. Steven Curtis Chapman said it best in his song entitled, "Fingerprints of God". Some of his lyrics are as follows: Never has there been and never again, Will there be another you fashioned by God's hand and perfectly planned

To be just who you are and what He's been creating since the first beat of your heart

Is a living, breathing Priceless work of art And I can see the fingerprints of God

When I look at you. I love that song! God formed each of us in the womb and left his fingerprints on us. In Jeremiah 1:5, it says: "Before I formed you in the womb I knew you, before you were born I set you apart; I appointed you as a prophet to the nations." Isaiah 49:6 says this: See, I have engraved you on the palms of my hands; your walls are ever before me. Every time I look at my children, I see a masterpiece from God like none other. I am grateful for the gifts he has given me, even if it is just for a little while.

Prayer for today: *Heavenly Father, I pray that you will continue to watch over your children that you*

147

have placed in my hands to care for. Help me to be a better mother to them and instill your character in them daily. I thank you for the gifts you've given me. In Jesus' name, Amen.

Contentment/Peace

Inward Beauty

A few weeks ago, a girl came to our neighborhood to visit my son. They met in our local park and were both sitting at the picnic table. When I was out walking, I casually walked over and introduced myself. I asked her where was she from. She said that she lived 5-10 miles away and her mom just dropped her off. She had on lots of makeup, skin tight jeans, and a low cut t-shirt on. First impressions say a lot. I thought to myself, this girl is only 15 years old and she's starving for attention. I have to say though that I like her were one in the same. I wanted to be loved, not just liked at her age. I had no idea the concept of what real love was until I grasped the cross at age 40. I remember one time a man told me from our church that there was nothing sweeter than watching his wife fall asleep while reading her bible. When you have inner beauty, you respect your outward beauty. Your inner beauty shines from the fruit of the Holy Spirit that can only come through Jesus. In 1 Peter, 3:4 it says the following: Rather, it should be that of your inner self, the unfading beauty of a gentle and quiet spirit, which is of great worth in God's sight. I may have the gentle part down pat, but the quietness I am still a work in progress. When you have inner beauty, you are trustworthy in character. Proverbs 31:30 says the following: Charm is deceptive, and beauty is fleeting; but a woman who fears the LORD is to be praised. When you fear the Lord, you can't help but to honor him. He wants your heart, soul, mind, and strength. There is a song I remember singing in my grandparents church when I was little. It went something like this: Have thine own way Lord, have thine own way, search me, and try me master today. Mold me and make me after thy will. While I am waiting, yielded and still. If we die to ourselves and live for the Lord we will be beautiful not only on the outside but on the inside as well. Take a look in the mirror. Now, take a good long look. What do you see past the make up? I will tell you what God sees. He thinks you are beautiful just the way you are.

Prayer for today: *Heavenly Father, remind me that I shine from the inside outward always and that when I glow that light comes from your light within me! In Jesus' Name, Amen.*

Treasure in Heaven

Where is treasure found? So many people have different views on what treasure is to them. It could be diamonds, money, pearls, land, homes, or cars. To me I find my treasure is found in Jesus. If he is your treasure, then the material things don't mean as much. Nothing compares. In Matthew 6:21 it says the following: Wherever your treasure is, there the desires of your heart will also be. Why do people wear themselves out to get rich? It is only temporary. They will never have true joy. The pleasure will only last a moment. In Matthew 19:23 it says the following: Then Jesus said to his disciples, "I tell you the truth, it is very hard for a rich person to enter the Kingdom of Heaven. In the book of Mark, a man asks Jesus what must he do to have eternal life. Jesus asked him if he was following the commandments. The man replied that he was. Then In Mark 21 it says: Looking at the man, Jesus felt genuine love for him. "There is still one thing you haven't done," he told him. "Go and sell all your possessions and give the money to the poor, and you will have treasure in heaven. Then come, follow me." Then the man went away saddened. He didn't want to let go. In order to have true treasure, you can't idolize anything over Christ. Look at the woman who gave all she had. In Mark 12 when Jesus was at the temple, he observed the offerings. Many rich people put in large offerings. Then a widow came and put in two small coins. She gave all she had. In Mark 12:43 it says this: Jesus called his disciples to him and said, "I tell you the truth, this poor widow has given more than all the others who are making contributions. For they gave a tiny part of their surplus, but she, poor as she is, has given everything she had to live on." She knew where her treasure was! In Colossians 2:3 it says: In him lie hidden all the treasures of wisdom and knowledge. Do you long to find treasure that lasts? When you wake up is Jesus your first thought? Is the Lords day on Sunday his day? Do you give your first amount of income to him and not what is left over? Are you willing to lay down your possessions and follow him? Are you willing to give him more of your time? Are you willing to come to him with important decisions? Did you know that you are his treasure? In Deuteronomy 7:6 it says: For you are a holy people, who belong to the Lord your God. Of all the people on earth, the Lord your God has chosen you to be his own special treasure. Won't you let HIM be yours?

Prayer for today: *Heavenly Father, I pray that others will come to know you and realize that they have eternal security in you which is the treasure they are longing for. In Jesus' name, Amen.*

Sound Sleep

Have you ever wondered why some people can sleep so soundly and others wake at the drop of a hat? My oldest son can sleep through anything and sleep until noon. I on the other hand, am a light sleeper and wake up early in the morning. When I use to worry about something, I found it hard to sleep. In the book of Psalms 4:8 it says the following: In peace I will lie down and sleep, for you alone, Lord, make me dwell in safety. Knowing that the Lord is watching over me helps me sleep. In Psalms 3;5 it says the following: I lie down and sleep; I wake again, because the Lord sustains me. In the book of Matthew 8:24 it says the following: Suddenly a furious storm came up on the lake, so that the waves swept over the boat. However, Jesus was sleeping. He wasn't concerned there was a storm. He was not frightened. He was sleeping peacefully. In Mark 4:38 it says the following: Jesus was in the stern, sleeping on a cushion. The disciples woke him and said to him, "Teacher, don't you care if we drown?" He was not concerned they might drown. All he had to do was speak and the waves were calm again. I can tell you that for years I needed medication from man to help me sleep. Little did I know, that I had free medicine all along. It took me twenty years to find out that the soothing calming words of God would help me sleep. In the book of Proverbs 16:24 it says the following: Gracious words are a honeycomb, sweet to the soul and healing to the bones. The next time you can't sleep, why don't you try getting out God's word and listen to him put you to sleep. He's awake twenty-four hours every day and is always ready to listen and give advice. In Isaiah 26:3 it says the following: You will keep in perfect peace those whose minds are steadfast, because they trust in you. If you are at peace with yourself, you will be able to get a good night's rest. Turn all of your worries over to God in prayer and leave them with him to take over. Trust in him and have faith for him to calm your storm.

Prayer for today: *Heavenly Father, I pray that I will never sleep when I am not tired and will stay awake you call me too. I am thankful that you never sleep and are always awake to hear me when I call out to you. In Jesus' name, Amen.*

The Christmas Boot

In 1952 my mom was seven years old. Her dad was a carpenter building houses with her uncle at the time and her mom was a cafeteria lunch lady at the local school in Rural Georgia near Fort Valley. Times were very hard back then for my grandparents and mom. For Christmas she awoke to find a 2 inch high, red plastic boot filled with mixed nuts and candy. Beside it she got an orange. That was her only Christmas gift. Every year since then she has held onto the little faded red boot and has placed it out at Christmas time. It is a reminder to her of how poor they were, but yet were provided for by the Lord and they survived. In thinking of God provided, it brought to mind Adam and Eve. They needed clothing after they sinned and were without. In Genesis 3:21 it says: The LORD God made garments of skin for Adam and his wife and clothed them. God provided clothing. Take a look at the Israelites. God provided after they were brought out of Egypt on their journey to the promised land of Canaan, the people were worried where they were going to get their meal from. God provided "Manna", (sweet gum or resin type of bread) supernaturally from Heaven. In Exodus 16:29 it says: The Israelites ate manna forty years, until they came to a land that was settled; they ate manna until they reached the border of Canaan. They grumbled against God, and were worried they wouldn't have anything to eat. So, what did God do? He provided, to prove to them that he would take care of them. In Deuteronomy 8:3 it says: He humbled you, causing you to hunger and then feeding you with manna, which neither you nor your ancestors had known, to teach you that man does not live on bread alone but on every word that comes from the mouth of the LORD. He took care of His people! Same thing with Joseph and Mary. He sent an Angel as their GPS to direct them to Egypt to protect them from Herod. In Matthew 2:13 it says: When they had gone, an angel of the Lord appeared to Joseph in a dream. "Get up," he said, "take the child and his mother and escape to Egypt. Stay there until I tell you, for Herod is going to search for the child to kill him." God provided shelter! In Matthew 6:31-33 it says: So do not worry, saying, 'What shall we eat?' or 'What shall we drink?' or 'What shall we wear?' For the pagans run after all these things, and your heavenly Father knows that you need them. But seek first his kingdom and his righteousness, and all these things will be given to you as well. My mom grew up happy even though her parents were struggling. She was happy to get the Christmas boot. She didn't grumble, and she didn't complain. Times were hard, but God always provided because her family put their trust in Him, kept strong in their faith, and lived a Godly life to the best of their ability. If you only got a Christmas boot this year, would you be content?

Prayer for today: *Heavenly Father, forgive me of my complaining, grumbling, and discontentment. Help me to know that no matter where I am in my life and hardships I go through, that you are watching over me and will provide for my family. Thank you Father for your blessings. In Jesus' name, Amen.*

Inside Out

Today I looked all over for my favorite sweat pants. I couldn't find them, so next best thing was my husbands. He had an old "Go Blue" Michigan sweatshirt that I pulled out of his dresser. I put it on, and immediately I looked like I was a Yankee girl rooting for her Northern team! If someone saw me out shopping today, they would have thought the same thing. Underneath, inside though, the real me was born in Athens, Georgia. I'm a Georgia Bulldog fan through and through. First impression from the cashier though , was that I liked Michigan. Isn't that the same as Christians vs. non-Christians? How do you tell what's on the outside matches up with what's on the inside? I can talk to someone who dresses nice, and talks nice, but on the inside they are bitter, unforgiving, or maybe even prejudice. Their inside does not match their outside. In the Bible in Matthew 23:25 it says: "Woe to you, teachers of the law and Pharisees, you hypocrites! You clean the outside of the cup and dish, but inside they are full of greed and self-indulgence. In order to be a Christian you must have a changed heart in order to take on the characteristics of Jesus Christ. If you took a glass that was dirty inside and outside, and only washed the outside clean, the inside would still be unclean. Once we accept Jesus by faith as our savior he deposits his Holy Spirit inside us to take on his Character. Galatians 5:22-25 says: But the fruit of the Spirit is love, joy, peace, forbearance, kindness, goodness, faith-fullness, gentleness and self-control. Against such things there is no law. Those who belong to Christ Jesus have crucified the flesh with its passions and desires. Since we live by the Spirit, let us keep in step with the Spirit. It really doesn't matter what's on the outside, it's that you show the love of Christ and set a good example wherever you go. Adrian Rogers once quoted, "We ought to be living as if Jesus died yesterday, rose this morning, and is coming back this afternoon." Can people tell what team you're on, by knowing your heart and your actions? Or, do you have to wear a shirt that says it? I want people to know that I love Jesus everywhere I go no matter what I'm wearing on the outside. His love comes from the inside out.

Prayer for today: *Heavenly Father, thank you for*

teaching me your character so that I can set an example wherever I go. If I stumble, pick me up and place me right back on your path. In Jesus' name, Amen.

Roses

I love roses, don't you? My grandmother's favorite flower was yellow roses and so is mine. I've tried to grow roses and they are very tricky. It seems there are more thorns on the rose bush than the rose when I try to grow them. It's such a beautiful flower and it seems it is always given to someone special out of love.

I love to see roses wrapped around an arbor in the spring and summer. I have heard that the Biltmore garden in Asheville, NC is very pretty in the springtime. Maybe someday my family will get to see it in full bloom. Some of the roses on the estate are from the ones that George Vanderbilt purchased in 1895. How do they survive that long? The rose is considered the most perfect flower. Women love to get roses not only for their beauty and fragrance, but because it symbolizes perfection. Jesus is referred to the "Rose of Sharon" as an analogy. Sharon was a place in Palestine that was considered a plain or valley full of wild flowers known for their beauty. In the book of Solomon 2:1, it says, "I am the rose of Sharon, and the lily of the valleys." Solomon's bride was stating this. She was choosing a perfect flower to describe herself to her groom. She was giving herself to her husband.

When Jesus comes back for his church, he will be like the rose of Sharon. He is perfect and he will be coming back for His bride. What an awesome analogy for God to use as Jesus being the perfect flower and wanting a relationship with us. Normally, we give a beautiful rose to the person we love. Jesus is the rose to be given, I think because He is perfection. Thorns were not with creation in the beginning. They came with the fall of man when man first sinned against God. When Jesus was crucified in the book of Matthew 27:29, it states "And when they had platted a crown of thorns, they put it upon his head, and a reed in his right hand: and they bowed the knee before him, and mocked him, saying, Hail, King of the Jews!" What a picture of Jesus as the perfect raised taking on our sin as the thorns pierced his head. His blood washed over all the thorns. Jesus the "Rose of Sharon" washed my sins away and returned me to the Garden of Eden. What a sweet aroma!

Prayer for today: *Heavenly Father, help me to always be a pleasing aroma wherever I am today, because you are inside of me. In Jesus' name, Amen.*

Resting in Righteousness

What is righteousness anyway? You hear people say, "Oh they are self righteous." Others say they are clothed in righteousness.. Webster's defines self righteousness as a "holier than thou attitude," meaning you may think you are above God. Prideful. My dictionary concordance in the back of my bible says the definition for righteousness is this "acting in a morally correct manner; correct by divine declaration." "Clothed in His righteousness" would mean to me that we are sealed once who fully surrender our lives to Christ. We may sin and step out of line, but we are forgiven after repentance because of the blood of the lamb. Psalm 132:9 says "may your priests be clothed with righteousness, may your saints sing for joy." Once you have the Holy Spirit in you, it's hard to not know when you mess up. We have a greater chance, though, of staying on the right chosen path when we are filled with the Spirit than when we are not. Psalms 89:14 says "righteousness and justice are the foundation of your throne; love and faithfulness go before you." Proverbs 11:5-6 says the opposite about those who are not walking right with God – "the righteousness of the blameless makes a straight way for them, but the wicked are brought down by their own wickedness. The Righteousness of the upright delivers them, but the unfaithful are trapped by evil desires." Proverbs 11:8 says "The righteous man is rescued from trouble, and it comes on the wicked instead." Proverbs 11:18 says "the wicked man earns deceptive wages, but he who sows righteousness reaps a sure reward."

Righteous people attain life while on earth and are filled with joy because the Lord blesses them. They do not fear death because they walk with God while living a godly life. They rest in knowing their eternity is with Jesus, God's gift to them. Those who are not saved will miss out on real joy and satisfaction on earth. Charles Spurgeon once wrote about the righteous being safe. He wrote "The man that is sheltered in his God — a man that dwells in the secret places of the tabernacle of the Most High, who is hidden in his pavilion, and is set upon a rock, he is safe; for, first, who can hurt him?" My answer is no one because I am resting in righteousness and I hope you are too!

Prayer for today: *Heavenly father, may You cleanse me from all unrighteousness. May You make my pathway pure. When I mess up, discipline me and get me back on track for Your glory. Make me so in tune with You that I hear you speak so that I stay focused in You and You alone. Thank you for giving me rest in rough waters. In Jesus' name, Amen.*

When the Wind Blows

While standing outside this morning early with our dog, Zoe, I couldn't help but notice how windy it is. I looked at our neighbor's house and their flag was swaying so fast. The trees were almost in unison it seemed like they were dancing together. I remember a movie a long time ago about a man with a brain tumor. The only thing that calmed his brain down was sitting outside and watching the wind blow the trees. Sometimes the wind can be scary in a storm. Sometimes the wind can bring a breath of fresh air. I used to love to stay at my grandmothers in the summer time and help her hang out clothes on the clothes line. When a good wind would blow, the sheets would flap back and forth and I would run in between them. That was a good memory. The bible says in Mark 4:39 the following: And he arose, and rebuked the wind, and said unto the sea, Peace, be still. In addition, the wind ceased, and there was a great calm. I remember reading in the book of Jonah last night to my son in chapter 1:4 it said, "but the LORD sent out a great wind into the sea, and there was a mighty tempest in the sea, so that the ship was like to be broken." God controls the wind. He can make a mighty whirlwind come about in a matter of seconds or he can choose to bring about a nice breeze on a hot summer day. The word wind is mentioned 123 times throughout the bible. It is a significant form of God's creation. In the book of John 3:8, it says the following: The wind blows wherever it pleases. You hear its sound, but you cannot tell where it comes from or where it is going. So it is with everyone born of the Spirit." The Greek word for spirit is wind. Isn't it amazing how so many believers can share the same spirit of God anywhere at any given time? Just like the wind may blow in the east, it can also blow in the west at the same moment. So can the Holy Spirit. Just like the wind, you can't see it but it is real. Do you believe in the wind even though you can't see it? It's just as easy to believe in the Holy Spirit. Close your eyes and feel the fresh wind blow, and calm your inner being.

Prayer for today: *Heavenly Father, help me to be a light in the darkness and fill me with your holy spirit wherever I go so others can feel your presence and come to know you. In Jesus' name, Amen.*

God's Got Something Better

One day at church while patiently waiting for a parking space just as we were about to pull in, someone else backed into the space! We then were in search for another one and the same thing happened. We were about to lose our cool, then suddenly a lady backed out and we found the perfect one. It was actually closer to the church and had less walking time than the two other spaces. God had something better and we didn't even know it. Isn't that the way it is with a lot in our life? We think we are missing opportunities, but usually God has something better in store for us. Sometimes in our life we think this is it and this is where God wants me. I've finally found where God wants me to serve him. Then out of nowhere something goes haywire and your right back at square one. Or maybe it might just be a job. You're probably thinking, why didn't I get that call back after the interview about the position? It's because God says wait, he's got something better! We have to pray about it, trust in his timing, and wait. God never closes a door unless it needs to be closed. In the book of Psalms 33:20 it says the following: We wait in hope for the LORD; he is our help and our shield. It's kind of like when you tell your children to wait until their food cools down because it's too hot and

163

they will get burned. We know what's best for them and God knows what's best for us! In Hebrews 11:40 it says the following: since God had planned "something better" for us so that only together with us would they be made perfect. If you're tired, worn out, and you just don't know which way to turn seek him, and wait patiently. I know that's a hard prescription order to fill. I have a huge battle with patience. The old saying though is good things come to those who wait. I want good things, don't you? Just when you're at your wits end, that's when he reveals himself so you can look at the whole picture and thank him for your unanswered prayer. I can look back on my life and think how many times I prayed for things that "I" thought was best for my life and was totally wrong. Gods plan for my life was something better. In Jeremiah 29:11 he tells us he knows the plans he has for us to give us hope and a future. He is the lead architect, now sit back and wait for the finished product that he will construct in your life!

Prayer for today: *Heavenly Father, I pray that I will not fall back into my old way of thinking where I was once in control. I pray that you will always keep me focused on you and what you have planned for my life. In Jesus' name, Amen.*

Humility

Shoes

Have you ever walked a mile in someone's shoes? Look around you. You may be sitting next to someone who recently lost a loved one to cancer. Alternatively, maybe you're out walking and pass someone who just lost their job. Recently on face book, someone posted about a couple who just lost their home to a house fire. Can you imagine losing your most valuable possessions and starting over from scratch? What if we were able to look at peoples shoes and they told a story. Some shoes are worn and tired. Some shoes are shiny and new. Have you ever heard the song called, "The Christmas Shoes" by New Song? A little boy wanted his sick mother to have the best shoes his money could buy to wear because he knew she would be meeting Jesus soon. A few years back I had the opportunity to visit the Holocaust Museum in Washington, D.C. and I have to tell you it left a mark on me. There was a long corridor hallway that you walked down and surrounding you in a glass case piled high were hundreds of shoes. They were the shoes worn by men, women, and children who lost their lives in the concentration camps. Can you imagine the pain and anguish they suffered? It reminds me of the picture of the soldier who has died and the only thing left is his boots, rifle, and helmet and the United States Flag flying in front of it. I can't imagine the fear of the soldier who walked in those boots and where they might have traveled.

I also think of the dirty sandals that Jesus and his disciples must have worn from traveling from town to town on foot. In the New Testament, it talks often about washing feet. In John 13 Jesus washed his disciple's feet. He wanted to show them true humility. Being humble before someone is letting go of all pride. In James 4:6, it says the following: But He gives a greater grace. Therefore it says, "God is opposed to the proud, but gives grace to the humble." Have you ever washed anyone's feet and thought about while doing it where that person has been and the miles they've traveled through trials and tribulations in their life? Until last year, I had never done that. When I washed my Daddy's feet and read to him John 13 and why Jesus said for us to do this and we will be blessed; I had no idea how many emotions were involved in that act of humility. If you ever want to experience true humility, start looking a little lower. The shoes always tell a story.

Prayer for today: *Heavenly Father, I pray that we will always desire to walk in your ways. In Jesus' name, Amen.*

Grace in Groceries

Yesterday as I was grocery shopping, I ran across an older lady who seemed puzzled over what batteries to buy. As she stood there, I knew I had to help her so I stopped to assist her. She was older in years, but she was beautiful and not just on the outside. As I rounded the corner we met again and talked about our pets and then laughed over the cheese puffs. Then it dawned on me! I had met her briefly, once before. She was one of my very good friend's mom! As I told her who I was, she opened up to me about quitting smoking, her sister recently dying, that she came from a family of ten siblings, and it seemed she just needed someone to lend an ear. I invited her to our church and shared with her about God's word and His Holy Spirit. I helped her at the checkout and made sure the bagger was going to walk her to her car. To be honest, I enjoyed her company and was so glad our paths crossed!

Have you ever been in a similar situation? I think of the Good Samaritan story in Luke 10; about the man who was robbed, stripped naked and left for dead. A priest passed him by on the road, a Levite passed him by and then the Samaritan came along! The Samaritan helped the man, bandaged his wounds, took him to an inn and paid for his stay in order to heal. In Luke 10:36 -38 it says "'Which of these three do you think was a neighbor to the man who fell into the hands of robbers?'" The expert in the law replied, "'The one who had mercy on him.' Jesus told him, "'Go and do likewise.'"

We are called to love our neighbors as ourselves and not to just pass them by. "Therefore, as God's chosen people, holy and dearly loved, clothe yourselves with compassion, kindness, humility, gentleness and patience." (Colossians 3:12) If we put on these characteristics daily, what a light we would be to others who need a glimmer of hope! Charles Spurgeon once wrote "Your own heart will not prosper unless it is filled with intense concern to bless your fellow men." We have to put others before ourselves in order to fulfill our purpose in this life. When we do, God sees it and will reward us with blessings in doing so. 1 Samuel 26:23 says "The Lord rewards everyone for their righteousness and faithfulness."

Prayer for today: *Heavenly Father, I pray that You will continue to nudge me to help others and to know when they need it. Put someone in my path today that needs to be loved on by You. In Jesus' name, Amen.*

Through His Eyes

While in a recent hospital stay my son and I were invited to attend a mini concert to listen to two guys playing songs with guitar. Other patients were there. They asked for song request and a little girl named Haley had one. They invited her to come and sing while they played. She seemed to be around age ten. She was battling cancer. She was broken out all over with a rash from her chemo and had very little traces of blonde hair and wore a patient mask. The song she sang to the top of her lungs was, "The Climb" by Miley Cirus. Some of the lyrics go like this: "There's always gonna be another mountain. I'm always gonna wanna make it move. Always gonna be a uphill battle. Sometimes I'm gonna have to lose. Ain't about how fast I get there, Ain't about what's waiting on the other side. It's the climb." As I got choked up inside, all I could do was pray. She didn't care what she looked like, she knew she was determined and beautiful inside and out to me! 1 Peter 3:3-4 says "Your beauty should not come from outward adornment, such as elaborate hairstyles and the wearing of gold jewelry or fine clothes. Rather, it should be that of your inner self, the unfading beauty of a gentle and quiet spirit, which is of great worth in God's sight." The image of her beauty will be etched in my memory for a while. When God looks at you, what does He see? The bible tells us that we are fearfully and wonderfully made. It says that the Lord delights in those who love Him. When we gaze on God's glory, His radiant light shines through us! 1 Samuel 16:7 says "But the LORD said to Samuel, 'Do not consider his appearance or his height, for I have rejected him. The LORD does not look at the things people look at. People look at the outward appearance, but the LORD looks at the heart.'"

To me a person's character reveals their beauty. Ruth Bell Graham was an amazing woman to me. She left her dream of joining the mission field abroad and supporting her husband's ministry instead for sixty-three years. She wrote fourteen books and a lot of poetry. When she passed away and went home to Heaven, her daughter Ruth wrote "Jesus was her center. We knew that Jesus was the reason she was the way she was, but she didn't preach it. She just simply lived it." Her other daughter, Anne Graham Lotz said "It was her love for the Lord Jesus, with whom she walks every day, that made me want to love Him and walk with Him like that." When people look at you, do they focus on your outward or inward beauty? Ruth Bell Graham's beauty was the life she lived for Jesus and how she touched others with His character. Looking through the eyes of Jesus at others, you will be able to see beauty in everyone no matter what they are going through or look like.

Prayer for today: *Heavenly Father, I pray that I will stay focused on the task You have laid out before me. I pray that I would see people through Your eyes in a loving matter and touch them and leave an impact for Your glory. In Jesus' Name, Amen.*

To Give or Not to Give

When it's Christmas Season and that means everywhere, you look people are in a mad rush! They are looking for that perfect gift, perfect toy, decorations, and food item. What if we slowed down America just a bit and took a good long look at why we are in such a rush anyway. I think the media has something to do with it for sure. Right after Halloween the very next day, if you turned on the television you would find at least one retail Christmas commercial. Seems like we just skipped over Thanksgiving all together. I heard a song the other day, by Matthew West entitled, "Give this Christmas Away". When Matthew West was interviewed about the song, he said the following: West explains in a press release, "What it means to me to 'give this Christmas away' is to pause long enough to look at the world from a perspective of 'How can I help? How can I give? How can God use me to help meet the needs of somebody else this Christmas instead of just checking off the list of everything I want?'" It made me think. What if we did give up our Christmas for ourselves and give it to those in need? We could stop poverty almost in its tracks! Look at some of the people in the Bible that gave. In Mark chapter 12 it talks of the widow who gave all she had. In Mark 12:43-44 it says this: Calling his disciples to him, Jesus said, "Truly I tell you, this poor widow has put more into the treasury than all the others. They all gave out of their wealth; but she, out of her poverty, put in everything—all she had to live on." What about the story of the good Samaritan? A man had been attacked by robbers and left for dead. Two people walked right by him without even helping! (one was a Priest) In Luke 10:33-35 it says: But a Samaritan, as he traveled, came where the man was; and when he saw him, he took pity on him. He went to him and bandaged his wounds, pouring on oil and wine. Then he put the man on his own donkey, brought him to an inn and took care of him. The next day he took out two denarii[e] and gave them to the innkeeper. 'Look after him,' he said, 'and when I return, I will reimburse you for any extra expense you may have.' He gave his time to a man in need. If we all made up our mind to really give this year, this world would be such a better place! A smile, opening a door for someone, visiting others who don't have any family nearby, sending cards, calling someone to let them know you care, are just a few examples of the love of Jesus we can share with others. So, that brings us to our question. To give or not to give? Giving is always rewarding, and if you give of yourself then one day someone will give back to you when you least expect it!

Prayer for today: *Dear Heavenly Father, teach me your ways so that I can have a loving, and giving heart like yours. Help me to see others through your eyes so that I don't pass anyone by in need that crosses my pathway. In Jesus' name, Amen.*

Undefineable

Have you ever lost something valuable and searched everywhere until you found it? My husband gave me diamond earrings for our anniversary several years ago. They are the kind with screw backs on them so you won't lose them. Well, leave it to me to lose one! I was afraid to tell him, so I searched everywhere. I looked on the floor, on my bathroom counter and had that sick feeling in my stomach. Suddenly, I had an idea to look in the bed. When I did, I found it on my pillow! Talk about a sigh of relief. I remember one time our Pastor lost his bible. He had placed it on his car and drove off. I can't imagine losing mine, so I know he must have felt sick. Years of notes throughout it and then all of the sudden it vanished. Luckily someone found it on the side of the road and it was returned. In Luke 15:8-10 it says this "Or suppose a woman has ten silver coins and loses one. Doesn't she light a lamp, sweep the house and search carefully until she finds it? And when she finds it, she calls her friends and neighbors together and says, 'Rejoice with me; I have found my lost coin.' In the same way, I tell you, there is rejoicing in the presence of the angels of God over one sinner who repents."

What about the parable of the lost son? Or the lost sheep? When the son came back home after spending all of his money, his father wasn't mad, and instead through a huge party and welcomed him with open arms. When the sheep wandered off the shepherd left the ninety-nine and went looking for the one that was lost. When he finds it he tells all of his friends and is so grateful. In Luke 15:7 it says "I tell you that in the same way there will be more rejoicing in heaven over one sinner who repents than over ninety-nine righteous persons who do not need to repent." Charles Spurgeon once wrote about these three parables. He wrote, "The truth here taught is just this—that mercy stretches forth her hand to misery, that grace receives men as sinners, that it deals with demerit, unworthiness, and worthlessness; that those who think themselves righteous are not the objects of divine compassion, but the unrighteous, the guilty, and the undeserving, are the proper subjects for the infinite mercy of God; in a word, that salvation is not of merit but of grace." The value that God places on each of our lives is undefinble. We are precious to Him and are worthy. He rejoices over repentance and coming to know Him through His son Jesus!

Prayer for today: *Dear Heavenly Father, I pray today for my family and friends who are lost and need to come to know You as their Lord and Savior. In Jesus' name, Amen.*

Leading Like Geese

Did you know that when a flock of birds fly south, they are in a "V" shape for a reason? They take turns leading due to wind resistance. Research has revealed that as each bird flaps its wings, it creates an uplift for the bird immediately behind it. By flying in a "V" formation, the whole flock adds at least 71 percent greater flying range than if each bird flew on its own. Whenever a goose falls out of formation, it suddenly feels the drag and resistance of trying to go it alone. It quickly gets back into formation to take advantage of the lifting power of the bird immediately in front. Geese also go on an eating frenzy prior to the winter to store enough fat for the long journey. They prepare themselves then work as a team until they get to their destination. I would like to think when they honk, it tells the one in front to keep going and gives encouragement. Seeing the geese and how they work together made me think of Christians pulling together to spread the love of Jesus and fellowshipping with one another. 2 Corinthians 13:14 says "May the grace of the Lord Jesus Christ, and the love of God, and the fellowship of the Holy Spirit be with you all." Acts 2:42 says "They devoted themselves to the apostles' teaching and to fellowship, to the breaking of bread and to prayer."

We as Christians lift each other up in order to encourage and equip one another to fulfill God's plan. I recently volunteered in our community making sandwiches and distributing clothing to low-income families. I was concerned about no one showing up to help me and didn't think I could do it all alone. I prayed for God to send the help and He did in a huge way! Several volunteers came and we always were able to be the hands and feet of Jesus and get the job done by being a team. John Maxwell said, "People come together as teams, peers work together, and they make progress because they want the best idea to win." Did you know that geese look after each other as well? When a goose gets sick, or is wounded by gunfire and falls out, two other geese fall out of formation and follow it down to help and protect it. They stay with the goose until it is either able to fly again or dead, and then they launch out on their own or with another formation to catch up with their group. I think we can all learn a lot from geese. Who are you lifting up today? Who are you helping? Who are you mentoring?

Prayer for today: *Dear Heavenly Father, please give me a burning desire to help those in need. Give me Your eyes, ears, and heart so that I am constantly aware of my surroundings in order to share the Your love. In Jesus' name, Amen.*

Angels Unaware

Yesterday, I had a lady knock on my door. Before I could even talk to her good she was crying. She was selling something like a magazine subscription, but she couldn't get past telling me of the tragedy of her son. I invited her in and we sat at my kitchen table. She showed me a picture of her son. Tears welled up as she stated he was in the wrong place at the wrong time. He was shot in the back and she buried him not long ago. She told me he was from Virginia. She moved here to make a better life and send money back home for her other son. Was this all a ploy to get money? I have no idea. I didn't give her any money. You see she was hungry. I gave her a bag of groceries. She asked me for a small Bible. I offered her a big one, but she didn't want it as it was too heavy to carry with her every day she said. All I had were big ones, but I did give her a book I had published. I knew that might bring healing to her, as there is scripture all throughout it. We sat and prayed for a while, and the tears came streaming as we held hands. She said, I'm tired. I asked her if she knows Jesus? She said she did, but the enemy won't let her rest. I gave her scripture, encouragement, and showed her love to the best of my ability. She left my house with a smile. No sooner than I watched her leave, she vanished. How was I to know if I was being tested? In Hebrews 13:2 it says: Do not forget to show hospitality to strangers, for by so doing some people have shown hospitality to angels without knowing it. I have some neighbors that said that Ms. Mona knocked on their door too and they gave her donations. I hope she was not after money. If she was, she fooled me but she only got love and groceries from me. I pray that she will find strength and not grow weary. In Isaiah 40:29-31 it says: 29 He gives strength to the weary and increases the power of the weak. Even youths grow tired and weary, and young men stumble and fall; but those who hope in the LORD will renew their strength. They will soar on wings like eagles; they will run and not grow weary, they will walk and not be faint. I will never forget Ms. Mona. Her eyes of weariness left a mark on my soul. She very well could have been an angel unaware of my knowing it.

Prayer for today: *Heavenly Father, help me to help others and see them through your eyes. In Jesus' name, Amen.*

Humility

Prideful

The Judgment Seat

Today I had the wonderful pleasure of sitting in a court room for two hours with my son in traffic court. You see, he received his first traffic ticket a few weeks back. While the judge came in, all eyes were on her. She stated what rights each person had in the room and that each person would be appointed an attorney on their behalf. My son was squirming. This was good for him to be there. He did not want to talk to his attorney because you could tell he didn't waiver or give an inch. He made it known up front that he had very little sympathy. I told Preston that this is exactly how it will be when we get to Heaven. He will have to go before the one and only judge, "God" and give an account for every single action in his entire life. This was a good hard lesson for him. He paid his fine with his own money and he took a defensive driving course that he paid for as well. What does the Bible say about God judging us after our last breath is drawn? In the book of Revelation 11:18 it says: The nations were angry, and your wrath has come. The time has come for judging the dead, and for rewarding your servants the prophets and your people who revere your name, both great and small— and for destroying those who destroy the earth." We will stand one day before His throne and either he will say , "Well done my good and faithful servant", or He will say, "Apart from me you rejected me, and I never knew you." I have loved ones who think they are saved, who are not saved, and some that don't care to get saved. Their salvation is not secure. Jesus cannot be their advocate on their behalf because they have rejected Jesus. I pray for family constantly, extended family, friends, and even people I don't know. Nothing could be sadder than hearing someone plea their case on the final judgment day without a free get out of jail card. God offers the free card through his son Jesus. He sent his son to pay our penalty so we wouldn't be condemned to Hell for all eternity. All you have to do is accept Him, realize you a sinner, ask him to change you and take control of your life. Once you do and it's your turn to stand in front of God, Jesus will say, "Oh yes, I know him or her. I paid their sin debt in full." Welcome to the banquet table. Come and sit and enjoy all I have prepared for you my child.

Prayer for today: *Heavenly Father, I pray that if there is anyone in my family that does not have a true relationship with you, that you would put Christians in their pathway. I pray that you would use someone to grasp their heart and cause a stirring in it to have the desire to start looking to you for all things. In Jesus' name, Amen.*

Devastating News

Yesterday, on our local news our community learned the tragedy of the loss of a little girl. She had been missing for the past three days. The local authorities found the seven year old girl in a dumpster. Her attacker abused her in the worst possible way then, killed her and threw her away like garbage. I can't imagine what the little girl's family must be going through right now. How could this happen? The first thought that comes to my mind is "Satan". In the bible in John 10:10, it says Satan comes to steal, kill, and destroy. Although he killed that sweet girl, she is in Heaven in the arms of Jesus. The attacker will be caught one way or another. He will pay for his wrong doing while here on earth, if not when he sits before God! In the book of Isaiah 66:6 it says the following: For with fire and with his sword the LORD will execute judgment on all people, and many will be those slain by the LORD. Unless this person comes to know and accept Christ as his savior before he leaves this world, he will pay the highest penalty before God. In Matthew 5:21 it says the following: You shall not murder, and anyone who murders will be subject to judgment.' Sounds like to me, it's going to get pretty hot! In Ezekiel 33:12 it says: "Therefore, son of man, say to your people, 'If someone who is righteous disobeys, that person's former righteousness will count for nothing. And if someone who is wicked repents, that person's former wickedness will not bring condemnation. The righteous person who sins will not be allowed to live even though they were formerly righteous.' In Job 14:5 it says: A person's days are determined;

You have decreed the number of his months

and have set limits he cannot exceed. God knows when and how we are going to die. Sometimes, He allows bad things to happen because we are a sinful fallen world. Does it mean he does not grieve? No. Look at when Lazarus died, Jesus wept. It was devastating news for him too, however, just as he raised Lazarus from the dead he raised himself so we could all have hope. In John 11:25 it says: I am the resurrection and the life. Jesus told his disciples in the upper room that he was leaving us peace through him. He left us hope through him. Even though, satan comes like a lion devouring in the worst way, the lamb of Jesus was slain and prevailed for our eternal life with him in Heaven. Christ overcame death and because of that our grief turns to hope.

Prayer for today: *Dear Heavenly Father, I pray for everyone today that has lost a loved one. I pray that they will find healing and comfort in knowing that you overcame death for us and will bring a sense of peace to our hearts. Thank you Father for your love, your forgiveness, and being our anchor through the storm. In Jesus' name, Amen.*

Lukewarm Temperature

While taking a shower after my husband this morning, I quickly found out that the water was lukewarm. I expected it to be nice and hot and was looking forward to waking up. When I realized I only had barely enough time to wash my hair, I

Prideful

quickly got out as fast as I could. What a disappointment to start my day off! Did you know, that God feels the same way toward us when we do not put him first? In the book of Revelation 3:16 it says the following: So, because you are lukewarm—neither hot nor cold—I am about to spit you out of my mouth. Ouch! We are to seek God with our whole heart willingly and try our best to live for Him. In 1 Chronicles 28:9 it says the following: "And you, my son Solomon, acknowledge the God of your father, and serve him with wholehearted devotion and with a willing mind, for the LORD searches every heart and understands every desire and every thought. If you seek him, he will be found by you; but if you forsake him, he will reject you forever. I think God wants more than five minutes of our time a day, or one hour in church once a week. He knows everything about you. Don't you think it's time for you to know him? Don't wait like I did later in life and look back and say, "I wasted twenty good years that I could have spent sharing the love of Christ with others". Are you on fire for the Lord? Do you have a desire to share his love with others? Or, do you get in a routine with the business of your job, kids activities, deadlines, television, computer, that your temperature is barely warm and there is no room for God? I have to admit, I myself get caught up in friends, computer time, and trying to keep my house in order, that I don't take out as much time as I should. It's a constant struggle and requires scheduling and much prayer!

Prayer for today: *Heavenly Father, I pray that you will help me make better use of my time in order to seek you first before anything or anyone. I pray that you will wake me up early to spend time with you before my house comes alive! I pray that you will help me to remember your word so I can use it to help others or fight off the enemy if needed. Thank you Father God for loving me and keeping me on fire for you! In Jesus' name, Amen.*

Prideful

From the Author

I can tell you that looking back over the last year God orchestrated these devotions. I had originally started writing them for another ministry and had hoped to reach orphan girls with them. God obviously had other plans. He kept waking me up night after night in the wee hours of the morning to write these devotions. I always heard Satan whisper in my ear the word, "doubt". I prayed for confirmation for continuation of writing them one night. The next morning I woke up and turned on my computer and received an email from a Pastor in India. He stated, "Greetings and Blessings in the name of our Lord Jesus Christ, Dawn. I ran across your blog this morning and wanted to encourage you to continue writing these as they are very good. I would like to use them in my ministry. May the Lord Bless and keep you and your ministry." That was my confirmation to continue this journey. I hope you enjoy them and they speak to you in a mighty way as they are all from the Lord to Glorify Him and Him alone.

Dawn